LIVING BETWEEN JOBS

Meditations When You're Looking for Work

D1569181

Harriet E. Crosby

Augsburg

MINNEAPOLIS

For Greg Brandenburgh,
former colleague, dear friend, swell guy

LIVING BETWEEN JOBS
Meditations When You're Looking for Work

Cover illustration by Brian Jensen, RKB Studios Inc.
Cover design by David Meyer
Text design by James Satter

Library of Congress Cataloging-in-Publication Data

Crosby, Harriet.
    Living between jobs : meditations when you're looking for work /
Harriet E. Crosby
        p.   cm.
    ISBN 0-8066-2753-0 (alk. paper)
    1. Unemployed—Prayer-books and devotions—English. I. Title.
BV4596.U53C76 1996
242'.4—dc20   96-22559
                                                                   CIP

Manufactured in the U.S.A.   AF 9-2753

00 99 98 97 96   1 2 3 4 5 6 7 8 9 10

6150

Contents

Introduction

As I write this I am still unemployed. I do not know when my unemployment will end, though I am doing my best to find another job. I wage a daily battle against fear and anxiety over an uncertain future. Doubts and questions fly out of control through my mind: Will my unemployment benefits last until I can find employment? How do my friends and family see me now that I don't have a job? What do I really want to do with my life? How will I keep busy and productive during my unemployment? And most of all, where is God in all of this? There are times when I feel utterly worthless, my self-esteem battered beyond recognition, because I define much of myself by what I do for a living. Yet I also know that I belong to God alone and that my true identity is in Christ. As a Christian, how do I live between jobs?

Chances are that if you are reading this you are unemployed (or someone you love is unemployed); or you are underemployed in your present job; or you are considering a career change; or you are thinking about leaving the security of a forty-hour work week to run your own business. Regardless of the circumstances regarding your present job or career plans, you know all about battling uncertainty, fear, and worthlessness. Although I wrote *Living Between Jobs* for Christians experiencing unemployment, the same grace, love, and spiritual growth is available to anyone coping with an uncertain job future.

Being unemployed or facing unemployment presents us with an opportunity for spiritual growth. If we take the time to look at ourselves and reexamine our relationship with God during this very difficult period, we can turn unemployment into a time of exciting spiritual transformation.

That was my reason for writing this book—to transform my experience of unemployment into a spiritual journey. I found that treating myself with the same love, respect, and dignity as Christ does has helped me to not only survive my unemployment, but to thrive and grow as well.

Living Between Jobs is a book of biblical quotations, meditations, and affirmations to help nurture bodies, minds, and spirits in battling anxiety and feelings of powerlessness. Focusing on a passage from the Bible, meditating on that passage, and then affirming ourselves every day is invaluable while between jobs. It helps us get in touch with the best in ourselves and Christ, who is at work in all of our lives. Experiencing Christ during this trying period of applying and interviewing for jobs is indispensable in keeping our spirits up and cultivating a positive attitude about the world around us.

Nurturing my soul in the presence of Christ helped me discover the *providence* of God. I began to read the Scriptures to understand how God cares for people: God gives us what we need to survive *and* thrive. God cares for us even when we can no longer care for ourselves. God shows us that in spite of our unemployment there is more than enough in our lives to make life worth living. God helps us discover Christ and build our future.

I experienced several phases in coping during my unemployment. My first reaction to losing my job was one of almost overwhelming loss. I spent several weeks feeling very alone and grieving the loss of my job. After the sadness came anger. I was angry at myself, the company I used to work for, former colleagues—and God. Confronting and admitting my anger ushered me into a phase of spiritual growth. I began to experience my faith from a a new perspective of strength discovered in weakness. Finally, I experienced moments of transformation, special moments when I could look in the mirror and see the image of Christ.

There are several ways to use *Living Between Jobs*. If you are a morning person, you may wish to begin the day reading the scripture verse and the meditation, and then carry the affirmation in your heart as you search for a new job. Or you may prefer to read the book in the evening, when the house is quiet and you can relax and apply the words to your life. *Living Between Jobs* can be used throughout the day, before a job interview or as you work on a résumé, or photocopy a reading and tape it somewhere convenient— on your computer, bathroom mirror, or refrigerator, for example.

For those of you who keep a journal, writing about the day's reading is another way of exploring the Bible quote, meditation, or affirmation as it applies to your situation. Christians can help each other when *Living Between Jobs* is used in small group settings at home or church. However you decide to use *Living Between Jobs*, may it provide you with the strength and light you need to walk with Christ and greet each day with joy and hope.

Experiencing Loss

**As he was walking along, he saw Levi son of Alphaeus
sitting at the tax booth, and he said to him, "Follow me."
And he got up and followed him.
—Mark 2:14**

To become unemployed is to experience loss. Our jobs were a significant part of our lives. We spent eight or more hours a day, five days a week (or more) at work. Many of us spent more time with our coworkers than we did with our families and friends. And most of us identified ourselves by what we did for a living. Suddenly we wake up one day without a job to go to anymore. We have lost a very important part of our lives. No wonder we experience sadness, grief, and even anger.

As Christians we follow Jesus. Following Jesus means experiencing loss because Jesus calls us out of the safety and security of the past into a new life. Surely Levi didn't leave the security of tax collecting without a twinge of regret. God can call us to new jobs, ministries, and careers—but that doesn't mean we don't mourn what we've left behind.

I didn't really experience the loss of my job until a couple of months after I left work. When I lost my job, my initial reaction was a feeling of relief. I spent the first several weeks of unemployment resting and recuperating. But one day it hit me—*I lost my job!* I felt almost overwhelmed by anger—anger at God, former colleagues, and the economy. A time of sadness followed. I was grieving at last. I needed a therapist to help me finish grieving. With her help I eventually closed the door on my old job, dried my tears, and felt free enough to see what Jesus might be doing in me to create a new life. I had walked through an open door into a time of growth and healing.

The new life I've experienced since then has not been easy. It's tough being unemployed! But I have developed a whole new way of looking at myself and what God is doing in my life, which pleases me. Allowing ourselves to feel anger and grief closes the door on our old lives and opens another door to new life in Christ.

*I can experience grieving the loss of my job when I am ready,
knowing that I follow Christ, who makes new life possible.*

Beyond Sorrow

And Jesus said to him, "Foxes have holes,
and birds of the air have nests; but the Son of Man
has nowhere to lay his head."
—Matthew 8:20

Sorrow and even anger over the loss of a job is entirely natural. Our work was important to us, or at least the paycheck or relationships with coworkers were. Now that we're out of work, the most natural thing in the world is to feel deep sadness or anger. It's important to remember while grieving the loss of a job that such feelings are temporary. When we choose to accept and express feelings of sadness, we'll find that such feelings have done their work and that it's time now to move on. As Christians we don't have the luxury of hiding in a nest or burrowing a hole of sadness to live in. When we refuse to acknowledge how we really feel over the loss of a job, anger and sorrow become a way of life. They are good feelings when they help us grieve and heal from significant losses, but they should not become our permanent home. We are meant to follow Jesus and move on with our lives.

There are other things we can do to ensure that sorrow doesn't become a permanent home. Perhaps the most important one is to take care of ourselves physically. Sorrow and anger are powerful feelings that have actual physical sensations—tense muscles, heaviness in the pit of the stomach, and difficulty in sleeping, for example. Taking a brisk walk, jogging, or working out at a gym or aerobics class can help us to physically express powerful feelings of grief and loss.

Accepting and expressing feelings of loss and taking care of our bodies ensures that we don't settle down into a lifetime of sorrow. Our only permanent home is the journey with Jesus.

I can grieve whatever losses I need to grieve today
so I can better follow Christ.

No Turning Back

Jesus said to him, "No one who puts a hand to the plow and looks back is fit for the kingdom of God."
—Luke 9:62

Denial is the great enemy of loss. It robs us of our right to grieve, to rant and rave, and to get on with life. Denial beckons us to look back and rewrite history—"Well, maybe that wasn't such a bad job after all" or "I'd still be working if . . ." Denial keeps us from pursuing the kingdom of God. Denial would have us overlook hard-won lessons learned, such as integrity, forgiveness, and our ability to see God at work in the world again.

Many of us know someone who has suffered a significant, life-changing loss through a divorce, a shattered career, the death of a loved one, or a major illness. Unfortunately, many of us may know people who continually refuse to accept their losses. Such people often lead tragic lives. I knew a woman whose career was irrevocably shattered during middle age. Rather than grieving the loss of it and letting go. She continued to look backward at her old life and became a bitter old woman.

"No one who puts a hand to the plow and looks back is fit for the kingdom of God." Unemployment forces us to confront our loss and gives us the opportunity to embrace it, beat the ground, howl at the moon—do whatever it takes to deepen our souls and expand our lives so we can get on with following Jesus.

Today I do not look back. My hand is on the plow, and by God's grace I get on with the business of following Christ.

Transforming Defeat

But Moses said to God, "Who am I that I should go to Pharaoh, and bring the Israelites out of Egypt?"
—Exodus 3:11

Like Moses, each of is a reluctant hero. While we live between jobs, God calls us to embark on our own hero's journey—a journey that mirrors the way of Christ, a journey that transforms defeat into victory. Moses knew he was no hero, and that the way out of Egypt would be filled with overwhelming obstacles.

Although it may be difficult to acknowledge now, our lives are also made richer by the obstacles life presents. When we face difficulties without denial or equivocation, we discover new reservoirs of character, strength, and courage as Moses did on his own hero's journey. Unemployment offers us the opportunity to transform defeat into victory. It's as though unemployment is our testing ground, forcing us to draw on spiritual, physical, and emotional resources we had scarcely realized before.

Confronting and accepting hazards and defeat, rather than practicing denial, shows us what kind of stuff we are made of—the stuff of Christ. We quickly learn to mobilize inner as well as outer resources. We draw on the love and support of family and friends. Suddenly, courage, strength, and hope are no longer psychological or spiritual abstractions, but real, daily experiences. And, when placed in the context of overcoming unemployment's many obstacles and all-too-frequent defeats, we no longer take for granted the small pleasures God gives us. And a hero is born.

Like Moses, I travel my own hero's journey today. Following the way of Christ, I draw upon my inner and outer resources to overcome obstacles, confront defeat, and celebrate my victories.

Courage to Risk

**David said further to his son Solomon, "Be strong
and of good courage, and act. Do not be afraid or dismayed;
for the Lord God, my God, is with you."
—1 Chronicles 28:20**

British author G. K. Chesterton once wrote, "The paradox of courage is that a man must be a little careless of his life even in order to keep it." Surely Chesterton had paraphrased the paradox at the heart of Christ's gospel—that we must be willing to lose our lives to save them. Living the Christian faith, a faith filled with paradox, takes courage. Courage empowers us to "just do it"—to take risks during risky times.

Anything worth doing harbors risk. People recovering from addiction often tell how they risked losing their old addicted lives to find new lives offering the possibility of healing and growth. Addicts and alcoholics know that they must risk losing their lives in order to keep them.

Living the Christian faith requires the courage to risk. Those of us who are between jobs take courage in the knowledge that God is with us. We courageously risk discovering who God created us to be instead of allowing ourselves to be defined by the work we used to do. We courageously risk receiving the many blessings God showers on us through family, friends, and the natural world around us instead of blaming ourselves, others, and God for our unemployment. We courageously risk moving forward with our lives one day at a time, instead of believing that unemployment will darken our lives forever.

I am a courageous person. The Lord is with me.

Waiting for the Lord

**Wait for the Lord; be strong, and let your heart
take courage; wait for the Lord!
—Psalm 27:14**

Living between jobs means living with a lot of uncertainty. Such uncertainty too often breeds fear—fear about money, fear about the search for a new job, and fear about the future in general. We do not have to be controlled by fear, however. We do not have to live in denial. We are living during a very uncertain time and our fears are real. But acknowledging our fears is not the same as letting them control us.

As we wait for the Lord, we can have courage because Jesus is Lord even over fear itself. Because we live in Christ the Lord, we refuse to let fear dominate our lives. Under the lordship of Christ, there is much to live for. During our unemployment, we learn new things about ourselves everyday. We find that the love of family and friends grows in value and importance to us. We discover beauty in the world around us that enriches our lives. And we trust that God is always at work for good in our lives.

How do we resist fear? By acknowledging its presence while courageously waiting for the Lord.

I can resist fear today because I wait for the Lord.

Naming Our Skills

**But you, take courage! Do not let your hands be weak,
for your work shall be rewarded.
—2 Chronicles 15:7**

We begin to think about making a career change most often when we believe our talents, skills, and abilities are no longer being appreciated or developed to their full potential. If we are unemployed, we sometimes fear that our skills may never be used again. But the truth is that each of us have talents and abilities developed during work we have done in the past, and we can take courage from that. Those skills are truly ours and no one can take our experience from us. Because we can claim our present and past skills, we know we can do many different kinds of work in the future.

Making a career or job change in our lives often requires great courage to launch into the unknown. Only fear keeps us trapped in jobs that stifle the best in us. Only fear paralyzes us when we are unemployed. But identifying clearly what we are able to do, culled from our repertoire of past abilities, arms us with the courage to seek out new and exciting opportunities—ones where we can apply familiar skills and develop new ones.

Sometime today, take out a sheet of paper and write, "I know I can live my dreams because I can . . ." and then complete the sentence by listing as many talents, skills, and abilities as you can. Let your memory and imagination join forces and try to fill up the page. When you have filled the page, put it in a place where you can consult it regularly and draw courage from it.

*Strengthened by years of experience, my hands are not weak;
and I know one day I shall be rewarded
again for my work.*

An Inventory of Success

Then the word of the Lord came to him, saying, "What are you doing here, Elijah?" He answered " . . . I alone am left, and they are seeking my life, to take it away." He said, "Go out and stand on the mount before the Lord, for the Lord is about to pass by."
—1 Kings 19:9-11

Being unemployed is often filled with disappointments. A few examples are rejection by potential employers, dwindling financial resources, or the perpetual search for a good job that just doesn't seem to be out there. In spite of our best efforts to find employment, disappointments still come, and we sometimes feel like Elijah alone in his cave.

But God responds to Elijah with "Go out." We can dwell in our self-imposed isolation, counting our disappointments one by one, or we can get out and can focus on the successes we've experienced in life, viewing each success as a gift from God. We can choose to focus on how successful we have been throughout our lives in our relationships with family, friends, and God, and in how we have grown as human beings as well as at whatever jobs we have held in the past. We can see how surprisingly successful we are right now, in spite of the disappointments that come with being unemployed. We can come to see that success is much more than having a job. Success in life is a gift from God, a rich gift that does not disappoint.

Write out an inventory today of all of the successes you've experienced at God's hand, including ones you've had during unemployment. Put this list in a place where you can refer to it again when you've been disappointed—it will remind you to focus on how successful God has made you.

I leave my cave of disappointments today to stand before the Lord my God as a success.

Positive Self-Talk

**Finally, beloved, whatever is true, whatever is
honorable, whatever is just, whatever is pure, whatever
is lovely, whatever is commendable, if there is any
excellence and if there is anything worthy of
praise, think about these things.
—Philippians 4:8**

Sometimes it's just too easy to think of the mistakes we may have made that brought about unemployment. Self-talk that begins with "If only I had . . .", "I should have known . . . ", "I'll never be able to . . .", and "I'm just no good at . . ." keeps us stuck in the past. Dwelling on errors, negative thoughts, mistakes, or regrets about the past only robs us of the energy to enjoy our present circumstances and move confidently toward the future.

We can choose to interrupt negative thinking with positive thoughts. Paul encouraged the Philippians to think about things that are excellent and worthy of praise. When we focus our thoughts on things that are lovely, truthful, pure, and gracious, negative self-talk about the past is banished. One way we can think about things worthy of praise is to choose a beautiful or meaningful image to replace negative, unpleasant thoughts about the past. Focusing even for a moment on a flower, a verse from scripture, or a sunset can open us up to the beauty surrounding us in the present. Sometimes we can interrupt negative thinking by spending a little time with a special friend who has a positive outlook on life. Or we can choose to nurture and comfort ourselves with a long walk in the park, a prayer, a trip to the museum, or whatever gives us pleasure in life. We have the power to interrupt negative thinking any time we choose and to find the strength we need to enjoy life in the present, and this gives us hope for the future.

*Today is filled with excellent things, worthy of praise,
and I will think on them and enjoy them.*

Facing Failure

**It is the Lord who goes before you. He will
be with you; he will not fail you or forsake you.
Do not fear or be dismayed.**
—Deuteronomy 31:8

During unemployment we occasionally wrestle with failure. We feel we failed when we lost our jobs, and we feel rejected. It usually takes a long time before we can accept our failures. But when we do, we must realistically face and accept them, knowing that God does not fail or forsake us.

I have a friend who was devastated by failure after she was fired from her job. Rather than deny her situation, my friend faced her failure and identified her behaviors that brought about being fired. She was determined to use unemployment to learn from her mistakes and grow from the experience. Two years later, she is running her own small business and is happier than I've ever known her to be. God did not forsake her, but instead lead her through failure to a better place.

It took two full years before my friend could see that God had not failed her. As we struggle with our feelings of failure during unemployment, we can be comfortable knowing that God never fails or forsakes us.

I can grow from my experience of failure because
God does not fail me.

A Kick in the Teeth

Saul got up from the ground, and though his eyes were open, he could see nothing; so they led him by the hand and brought him into Damascus. For three days he was without sight, and neither ate nor drank.
—Acts 9:8-9

Walt Disney once said, "You may not realize it when it happens, but a kick in the teeth may be the best thing in the world for you." That seems to have been Saul's experience on the road to Damascus. One minute he was on top of the world, at the height of his power, a man possessed by uncommon religious zeal. The next minute he got a spiritual kick in the teeth that left him as helpless as a baby. I imagine Saul stricken during the three days that followed, a man suddenly thrust, so it would seem, into the outer darkness.

You may be reading this after having recently been kicked in the teeth. You may have just lost your job, been rejected for a new job you really wanted, or spent another grinding day in a job that no longer holds your interest. You know that these experiences are extremely painful. But in spite of the pain try to remember that "a kick in the teeth may be the best thing in the world for you." Like Saul, you may be undergoing a positive life-changing experience.

A major disappointment often gets us to take a look at our lives from God's perspective and see the big picture. Perhaps the job we really wanted would have hurt us in the long run. Perhaps God is saving us for something much better. Saul could look back and see that his blindness was preparing him to see a whole new world. When we suffer painful experiences of rejection or failure, we can grow by searching for a new perspective—God's perspective—on situations, relationships, and life in general.

Today's kick in the teeth may be tomorrow's miracle.

Broken Hearts

**My flesh and my heart may fail, but God is the strength
of my heart and my portion forever.**
—Psalm 73:26

There are times during unemployment when our hearts are
broken by disappointment, failure, and rejection. The antidote to
a broken heart is love and trust. We can pick up the pieces and go on
when we know that our hearts are still working—we have not lost the
ability to love our family and friends. We trust that God comes to us
in their love for us.

Broken hearts are strengthened when we trust in the love and
support of others whose hearts have also been broken. I, for example, belong to a small support group of unemployed women. We call
each other on the phone and encourage one another when disappointment comes. We also meet socially on a regular basis to laugh,
gossip, complain, and have a good time. I have found that when my
heart is broken, meeting with these women and trusting in their care
and support is God's way of showing love for me. Attending a support group of other unemployed people shows us that God can heal
our broken hearts.

And broken hearts are strengthened by trusting in the goodness
of God, whose own heart was broken at the death of his Son. We
trust in the goodness of God every time we look into the eyes of
someone who loves us, every time we take a moment to appreciate
beauty in the world, and every time we identify one blessing during
the course of our day. It may not feel like our hearts will ever be
whole again, but when we trust in the love and care God has for us,
our hearts are already on the mend.

*My flesh and my heart may fail, but God is the
strength of my heart forever.*

Time Out

**On their return the apostles told Jesus all they had done.
He took them with him and withdrew privately to
a city called Bethsaida.
—Luke 9:10**

We all know how overwhelming unemployment can be. So much is at stake. Finding another job is often so intense that sometimes the magnitude of the task overwhelms us. At these times, we need to take a break, a time-out. The antidote to being overwhelmed is to relax, stand back, and get some perspective on the situation.

After the apostles' strenuous exertions on behalf of the gospel, Jesus took them on a kind of retreat to Bethsaida. But the crowds followed them to the city—and Jesus welcomed them.

God does not intend for us to *escape* unemployment, but instead to *deal with it* by finding a new job or career. When we are overwhelmed, it is only human to want to escape or to be magically rescued from our unemployment. But we all know that's not the way life works. With a little relaxation and showing ourselves some old-fashioned TLC, we can cope with our feelings of being overwhelmed, and we can return to grapple with the harsh realities of the world with renewed perspective and freshened spirits.

*When I am feeling overwhelmed, I can retreat for
a time before returning to the fray.*

Perfect in Weakness

**. . . but he said to me, "My grace is sufficient for you,
for power is made perfect in weakness."
—2 Corinthians 12:9**

I have a friend who is fond of saying jokingly, "Like Mary Poppins, I want to be 'practically perfect in every way.'" There is a little Mary Poppins in all of us, the perfectionist who invests a lot of energy in showing the world how she can do *everything* and have it all. Every part of the perfectionist's life appears happy—no sadness, no messes, no failures of any kind. Men often suffer from the Mary Poppins syndrome just as many women do.

The way of Mary Poppins, however, is not the way of Christ. A life of discipleship is a life of God's "power made perfect in weakness." We are made "perfect" (complete, whole, fulfilled) in Christ alone, not in keeping up an appearance of perfection. It is through failure, sadness, and life's general messiness that we experience the powerful grace of Jesus Christ.

Unemployment does perfectionists a great service—it helps us confront our weaknesses. Unemployment breaks the appearance of perfectionism and lets us simply be human. It's very hard to keep up the illusion of "being practically perfect in every way" while living between jobs. After all, if we were so perfect, we'd have a job. So we must all admit that we are human beings who occasionally experience failure. But we also experience love, joy, and a lot of other wonderful feelings as well.

As disciples of Jesus Christ, we are free to give up perfectionism to experience the power of Christ's grace made perfect in weakness. We are free to accept love, free to forgive, free to give love, and free from keeping up exhausting, and unrealistic expectations of ourselves.

*I am unemployed and I'm not perfect. I am a disciple of
Jesus Christ, who frees me from perfectionism.*

A More Excellent Way

But strive for the greater gifts.
And I will show you a still more excellent way.
—1 Corinthians 12:31

Unemployment shows us perfectionists how low our self-esteem really is. In our heads we hear, "If you're so perfect, why don't you have a job?" or "You lost that job and now you're nobody." Trying to remain a perfectionist while unemployed is extremely counterproductive. Perfectionism won't find us a job; it will only make us feel miserable about ourselves. And when we feel miserable about ourselves, the energy to get out there and look for work just disappears.

For perfectionists there is "a more excellent way"—love. In his letter to the Corinthians, Paul goes on to write extravagantly about *agape*, the kind of love God has for us. Love makes life possible; it is the gift of gifts. When we strive to follow after love, we hear in our heads, "You did the very best you could in that interview; now let it go into the hands of God." or "You have the best skills for that job—go for it!" This is the voice of mercy. When we strive after love, family and friends, potential employers, the whole world sees it. So when we listen to those voices talking in our heads, let us follow a more excellent way.

Today I follow the way of love and leave the rest to God.

God Is Our Security

**Like a swallow or a crane I clamor, I moan like a dove.
My eyes are weary with looking upward. O Lord,
I am oppressed; be my security!
—Isaiah 38:14**

I take great comfort in security. My job was the primary source of my security, and I took it largely for granted. My job offered me a steady income, a routine that shaped my days, and tasks I enjoyed doing. My life was on a fairly predictable track of gradual upward mobility. When I lost my job, all that seemed secure in my life disappeared with it. I felt as though my life had been derailed. Suddenly the world seemed like a very uncertain, even dangerous, place.

When I was secure in my job, I unconsciously developed a kind of tunnel vision about my life. My world was relatively confined to the particular line of work I was doing, and I rarely admitted new possibilities—especially where God was concerned. While I was working full time, I did very little writing. Once I became unemployed, I began to write and sell a few writing projects. Soon I had a little free-lance business going—not enough to live on, but enough to ease the strain of unemployment a little. My writing enabled me to explore my relationship with God in a much more focused way. Now I see that only God can be my security—not a full-time job, not a free-lance writing career.

I discovered that I must never again take my life or God for granted. With security and certainty absent, the Spirit has begun to flow again into my life with God. The possibility of expanding horizons and exploring new frontiers in work and life is deeply rewarding when God is our security.

*Today God is my security and I am open to the
movement of the Holy Spirit.*

The Gift of Anger

**Insults have broken my heart, so that I am
in despair. I looked for pity, but there was none;
and for comforters, but I found none.**
—Psalm 69:20-23

Anybody who has been through the experience knows that losing a job is a tremendous catalyst for anger. For me, it was as if somebody had amputated a limb without my permission. I was furious. However, I left the office that last day without showing how angry and hurt I was. Instead of honestly expressing my anger later in the privacy of my own home, I stuffed my anger deep inside. For months I refused to admit how angry I was, telling myself that getting angry now wouldn't do any good anyway. I finally realized that even Christians get angry. Although letting myself become angry wouldn't get my old job back, it sure might make me feel better now. Confronting my anger and expressing how angry I was to God began to help me let go of the past, bring some happiness to the present, and look forward to future employment.

Don't let anyone, especially that little voice we all carry inside our heads, deny you your right to be angry. God blessed us with the ability to get angry—it *is* a gift. Expressing anger at the appropriate people in appropriate ways is healthy. It is how we begin to heal the pain of being hurt by others. Maybe we go into a room and yell for a while. Maybe we consult a counselor or therapist for a time. Sometimes we have the opportunity to get angry with those who hurt us. Sometimes that is impossible, but still, we can tell God how angry we are (sometimes over and over again) instead of ignoring our feelings. When we realize we don't have to renounce our faith when we feel angry over the loss of a job, we are able to show God our feelings and move on with our lives.

God has given to me the gift of anger to express responsibly.

The Mask of Boredom

**For God alone my soul waits in silence,
for my hope is from him.
—Psalm 62:5**

It is easy for me to confuse silence and boredom. I fill the silence by watching TV, listening to music or the radio, and talking on the telephone because silence threatens me with boredom. Yet the psalmist writes that silence is the greatest expression of our hope in God.

G. K. Chesterton once said, "A yawn may be defined as a silent yell." During unemployment, we often experience boredom. When looking for work, we experience periods of low activity and we feel bored. But boredom is sometimes a mask for more powerful emotions. The yawn may in reality be a silent yell screamed by anxiety or anger.

It is natural that we occasionally feel angry or anxious during unemployment. After all, being unemployed is like living with a long-term crisis. But we don't have to live in continual anger, anxiety, or boredom. Instead, we can ask God what emotions we are really feeling that we would rather cover up. We can choose to let boredom drag on and on, sapping our energy and draining away our enthusiasm for life, or we can choose to wait in silence for God alone. Paradoxically, sometimes we can best honor the silence by talking to a special friend who is willing to listen, a therapist, counselor, or support group. Once such feelings are appropriately acknowledged and expressed, we are free to hope in God again.

Remember, God has blessed us with a full range of feelings—including anger and anxiety—that make life fulfilling. Boredom flattens life, reduces it to a yawn. In silence we can identify boredom as a signal to discover and express the rich emotional life that God gives to each of us.

*For God alone my soul waits in silence,
for my hope is from him.*

Putting Anger to Work

So the king said to me, "Why is your face sad, since you are not sick? This can only be sadness of the heart."
Then I was very much afraid.
—Nehemiah 2:2

Nobody I know enjoys unemployment. Each of us must occasionally battle depression, that "sadness of heart" that comes with unemployment.

Depression is often anger turned inward. The worst anger we can experience is usually the anger we turn on ourselves. Perhaps that is why Nehemiah was so afraid upon hearing the king's diagnosis. I sometimes catch myself telling myself, "If you weren't so lazy, you would have found a job by now" or "You're kidding yourself if you think you have any skills an employer could possibly want." These messages are not only angry, they are also fear creating and ultimately self–defeating. They rob us of energy and the ability to take constructive action in finding new work—and they result in depression.

We have a choice about what we can do with our self-anger, though. We can stifle it—turn it inward and risk exhausting ourselves with prolonged depression. Or we can admit that we are sad and angry with ourselves about being unemployed, and then channel all of that energy into constructive action. Nehemiah did this, and he lived to become a great prophet.

Each of us must decide the best, most constructive way to make our occasional bouts with anger work *for* us instead of *against* us. Finding another job can take all the energy we've got. To conserve it, we must stop all the angry self-talk and put anger to work for us.

When I am angry at myself for being unemployed, I can make
my anger work for me rather than against me.

Cultivating Hope

**So I turned and gave my heart up to despair concerning
all the toil of my labors under the sun. . . .
—Ecclesiastes 2:20**

Despair is the absence of hope. Despair happens when we become convinced of the absolute darkness of our circumstances.

Sometimes during unemployment we may be tempted to give up our hearts to despair and abandon all hope. When we are between jobs, it is possible to cultivate hope in our situation, like a small, fragrant flower in the desert darkness. Ecclesiastes, the Preacher, knew all about despair. "Vanity of vanities," says the Preacher, "All is vanity." Despair is the conclusion of fools because only fools jump to the conclusion that life is utterly hopeless. The old saying, "Where there is life, there is hope," is true. We combat despair by searching for hope.

Reasons for hope are all around us. Cultivating hope means paying attention to the smallest details of our lives. Hope lives in the faces of those we love. If we really look at those faces, we'll absorb the hope we find there. Hope also lives in the natural world. If we look at the beauty in our backyards and local parks, and really listen to the birds sing, we'll find reason to hope. If we let go of despair and open our hears, God's providence will work for good in our souls.

Too often we take for granted the faces of loved ones, the simple beauty of bird song, and the activity of providence. They seem like such small, easily overlooked aspects of our lives. But paying loving attention to these details cultivates hope for fulfilling employment.

*Hope is all around me. Help me to pay attention to
my life and cultivate hope today.*

Do Not Fear

But overhearing what they said,
Jesus said to the leader of the synagogue,
"Do not fear, only believe."
—Mark 5:36

Unemployment offers plenty of opportunity to experience fear. We are sometimes afraid we'll never be able to find work again; afraid we'll run out of finances; afraid we'll interview poorly and be rejected.

All too often we make an already challenging situation, such as unemployment, much more fearful and nerve-wracking because we launch ourselves into useless, and often dark, speculation about the future. The truth is that we just don't know what the future holds, so why do we scare ourselves with dire fantasies and predictions? The future is just as likely to hold good news for us. We may very well find satisfying work again; money may solve our troubles and we may not be rejected in our next interview. We just don't know.

Jesus told the leader of the synagogue, whose daughter had died, "Do not fear, only believe." Our future, and even death, belongs to God alone. Our future rests in the hands of a good and loving God who asks us only to believe.

We can't let useless fantasies about the future rob us of the energy we need to cope with the challenges unemployment presents us. We can't let dire predictions rob us of the joy life offers us now, in the loving faces of family, friends, and this beautiful world. All God gives us is the present moment—and the promise of Christ's return. Jesus tells us, "Do not fear, only believe."

Today I believe and will not be afraid.

Living in the Moment

**You know how to interpret the appearance
of earth and sky, but why do you not know how to
interpret the present time?
—Luke 12:56**

There really is no time like the present. Unemployment seduces us to rerun the past in our heads—how we lost our jobs or what was good about our work and what wasn't. And unemployment tempts us to question the future. Will there be enough money or when will our joblessness end? When we refrain from playing old tapes from the past or catapulting ourselves into future fantasies, we'll find that the present is a thrilling place to be. The present frees us to focus on and interpret each moment under the mercy of God.

Each moment we experience is our first and our last. Each moment is also forgiving because it offers the chance to make a fresh, new start. Living fully in the present doesn't mean we forget the past, only that we no longer obsess over past wrongs and mistakes. Each moment makes no promises about tomorrow, for we live only under the grace and mercy of Jesus Christ and are free to enjoy the present without worry over an unpredictable future.

Living in the moment makes living between jobs bearable. We do the best we can to find new employment by making the most of every moment of every day. And in every moment we let go of past regrets and future improbabilities. We are thrilled to be alive, to love, to live in the hope of God alone.

Today I live each moment under Christ's mercy and grace.

Out of Control

Jesus said to them again, "Peace be with you. As the Father has sent me, even so I send you." When he had said this, he breathed on them and said to them, "Receive the Holy Spirit."
—John 20:21-22

I am a person who likes to be in control. I take pride in working to get what I want out of life. But unemployment challenges my ability to be in control. I can no longer control a significant part of my life—work. Many times I have desperately wanted a job during an interview, but I could not make a company hire me. When I experience a lack of control over my life, I begin to feel overwhelmed, powerless, like a victim of forces I cannot control.

That is when I need the cool, gentle experience of the peace of Christ. God's peace comes from accepting that the Holy Spirit, breathed on me by the living Christ, is Lord of the universe. For those times when I feel out of control and helpless, the Holy Spirit leads me to accept responsibility for those things God has given me to change. Some things I can change and some things I cannot. For example, I cannot change the fact that I was rejected after my last interview. But I can change my attitude about rejection. I can discard the hurt and anger and turn to the healing light of the Holy Spirit. I can let the Holy Spirit guide me toward whatever exciting, new thing that may be just around the corner. My hurt and anger are natural reactions to rejection, but holding on to those feelings over a long period of time changes nothing and only results in cultivating a deeper sense of powerlessness.

It is possible to know the peace of Christ even during such a difficult time as unemployment. May the peace of Christ be near you today. Recite this prayer when you begin to feel overwhelmed by forces you cannot control.

God, through your Holy Spirit, grant me the serenity to accept the things I cannot change, the courage to change the things I can, and the wisdom to know the difference.

Life Plans

"Jesus is Lord."
—1 Corinthians 12:3

I am a natural-born planner. I feel most secure when I have a plan for the day, the week, the year—my whole life. Having a plan helps me to believe in the myth that I'm in control. Most days and weeks my plans work relatively well. But when I try to plan out longer periods of time, like my entire life, my plans rarely turn out as I expected.

Many of us have probably said at one time or another, "Wow. Life sure didn't turn out the way I expected." Unemployment has shown me that the career I planned to have the rest of my life may very well not continue. And this forces me to reevaluate my life plans. In fact, I'm forced to reevaluate all of my preconceived ideas about what life *should* be under the lordship of Christ. One of the most valuable lessons unemployment teaches is that life rarely goes according to plan and we cannot control very much. Only Jesus is Lord of our lives.

There is good news, however, in accepting the fact that we control so little. The good news is that we can stop playing god with our lives and trust the Lord to show and direct our steps to a new path. God calls us to lead responsible lives and to do the best we can in caring for ourselves and our families. But God asks us to confess that Jesus is Lord and to let go of any compulsively detailed life-scripts we've written. Living between jobs may be God's way of breathing some fresh air into our carefully planned lives and offering new possibilities, and opportunities, under Christ's lordship.

Jesus is Lord. Today I let go of all those old plans that don't work anymore. I ask God to breathe fresh air into my life now.

Enough for Today

And God is able to provide you with every blessing in abundance, so that by always having enough of everything, you may share abundantly in every good work.
—2 Corinthians 9:8

One of the many challenges unemployment offers us is to be satisfied with enough. We can learn that God has already given us enough and even more than enough of everything. Each day is sufficient to itself, and we must live one day at a time under the eyes of God, who provides for us.

I find seeking sufficiency during unemployment a special challenge. It is too easy for me to project into the future and imagine being unemployed for the rest of my life. It is too easy for me to focus on what I don't have, such as a job or disposable income. It is too easy for me to ignore the abundant blessings God provides, such as people who love me or the simple fact that I have survived another day. When I let each day be enough, and *more* than enough, God's peace overcomes any negative flaws I have. God's peace sustains me. Unemployment is not a pleasant experience, but I can trust God to provide me with enough of everything each day. Living between jobs offers me an opportunity for growing spiritually in the trust and hope that God will provide me with "every blessing in abundance."

We can identify how God has given us more experience during tough times. If we focus on God's providence today, every day will be sufficient unto itself.

Today I have enough. God provides me enough,
and more than enough, of everything.

Sanctuary

Jesus answered him, "Those who love me will keep my word, and my Father will love them, and we will come to them and make our home with them."
—John 14:23

We all need sanctuary during unemployment. We need a place where we can, for a time, lock out the competitive, rough-and-tumble world. We need a place that nurtures our bodies and spirits, strengthens us for another day.

The peace we need isn't necessarily a lack of noise or even a lack of conflict. Finding peace means experiencing wholeness, a sense that we are whole, complete people who have everything in God. Home is one important place where we can find peace in the assurance that Jesus comes to make his home with us. Jesus comes to make us whole. During unemployment it is important not to take our home with God for granted but instead to appreciate it as a source of comfort and blessing filled with the presence of Christ. We need to think of our home and ask, "How are my body and spirit nurtured and restored to the peace of Christ in this place?"

Now, more than ever, we need a home in Jesus. If we share our homes with others, we may have to balance interaction with family members with retreating for a time into a comfortable room by ourselves. Or perhaps we may find peace by caring for those who fill our homes. If we live alone, finding peace may mean regularly practicing hospitality. When we invite others into our homes, we find that relationships with them also nurture us. God has come home to you today. Seek God's peace.

Today God has come to make his home with me.
I seek Christ's peace.

Beautiful Things

**While he was at Bethany in the house of Simon the leper,
as he sat at the table, a woman came with an alabaster jar of
very costly ointment of nard, and she broke open the jar
and poured the ointment on his head.**
—Mark 14:3

Now that we are unemployed, chances are we're spending a lot more time at home. Our homes, of course, were very important to us while we were employed. But they are doubly important now that we are out of work. The physical surroundings of our home make a subtle, though very important, contribution to help define who we are during unemployment.

The verse about the woman pouring ointment on Jesus shows us that we must not overlook beauty in our surroundings. Just as the expensive ointment helped define who Jesus really was—prophet, king, messiah—so too beauty in our homes remind us that we are much more than workers. We are heirs to God's kingdom. Just as walking in a beautiful park can restore our spirits, so can the things we treasure in our homes. The poet Keats wrote, "A thing of beauty is a joy forever." We must appreciate the beautiful objects that surround us in our homes, for they are another source of nourishment for our souls.

Not long after I became unemployed, I created an herb garden in pots on my cottage deck, and it is a simple source of fragrant beauty to me. My garden reminds me there is more to my life than earning a living. Framed photographs of loved ones, grandma's china, a favorite chair, a bookshelf filled with books, lush house plants, or even matching towels in the bathroom may subtly remind you that you are an heir to God's kingdom. Savor the beauty of your surroundings and let your home nourish your soul.

*The beautiful things in my house feed my soul and
prepare me to greet another day.*

Hard Joy

**Let me hear joy and gladness; let the bones
that you have crushed rejoice.
—Psalm 51:8**

Joy is hard happiness. God's joy comes when we refuse to escape or deny the reality of a difficult situation. In Psalm 51, the psalmist does not deny his pain and anguish, yet he trusts in God's gift of joy. Joy unexpectedly pierces our lives when we work through a rough time in marriage, agonize over a teenager's behavior, or wrestle with living alone. God's joy comes from handling the hard, rough textures of real life.

Joy flares with a bright intensity during dark times, and unemployment is one of those times. Joy is a hard happiness that visits us when we confront the reality of being unemployed and then cope with it in the presence of God. There is joy in courage—courage to confront financial problems, handle difficulties in getting interviews, and work through the daily obstacles that come with any job search. There is joy in honesty—honestly exploring who we are, what we really want out of life, and what we need from loved ones. There is joy in having enough—being satisfied with what God gives us today to live on and love on.

God's joy is not pleasant. It suddenly breaks through hard reality knocking us breathless with its power and leaving us transformed. And we are changed by the knowledge that it's worth the struggle and pain of being unemployed to become more real—more deeply, intensely human.

*Today may be hard and rough, but I can know
the sharpness of God's joy in it.*

A Sense of Satisfaction

Satisfy us in the morning with your steadfast love, so that we may rejoice and be glad all our days.
—Psalm 90:14

When I was a teenager, one of the songs I used to listen to over and over again was "(I Can't Get No) Satisfaction" by the Rolling Stones. "I can't get no satisfaction" is a frequent refrain of modern life. It is a phrase that chooses to focus on all that is missing in life rather than the presence of abundance. It sums up our refusal to be satisfied with what we already have—God's steadfast love.

Those of us between jobs must fight the temptation of chronic dissatisfaction, which robs us of the energy to enjoy life. One way to cultivate a sense of satisfaction every day is to open ourselves to God's steadfast love. Satisfaction in the love of God alone is an inner response to our outer circumstances. We may be unemployed, but God loves us now more than ever:

- God has given us skills and abilities that are a source of pride.
- God regularly loves us through our relationships.
- God provides for us and guides us in all our efforts.
- God helps us survive another day.
- God strengthens us to do the very best we can to find work.
- God loves us through the beauty we find in the world.
- God is Lord over our health and well-being.
- God fills each day with blessings.
- God gives us enough for today.

The truth is we *can* get satisfaction even though we are unemployed. Our satisfaction comes from the steadfast love of God today and every day.

Today I am satisfied by God's love.

Starting Over

**"Truly I tell you, unless you change and become like
children, you will never enter the kingdom of heaven."
—Matthew 18:3**

I have a friend who is fond of reciting, "All change, even change
for the better, is processed as loss." In other words, all change means
leaving something behind even when it means gaining something
else. Jesus says that discipleship demands change. In a way, the
Christian life is a constant starting over—a constant returning to
childlike faith and trust.

Unemployment is about change and starting over. I woke up the
day after I lost my job feeling as though my life was ruined. I
believed I was a total failure. But after a couple of months I gradually
stopped defining myself exclusively by what I did for a living and
focused instead on seeing myself as a child of God. After several
interviews, I began to see the possibility that something really new
and good could come from losing my old job and beginning again.
In other words, the more I felt like a child of God, the better I felt.

Change demands accepting losses and discovering hope. We
gradually become stronger when we allow ourselves time to look past
what we lost and instead view ourselves as children of God, heirs
to God's kingdom. We have reason to hope. There will be many
possibilities our new life can offer. Change in the life of a Christian
may involve experiencing loss, but it can also involve experiencing
childlike faith and trust once again.

Today I am a child, loved by God and heir to the kingdom.

The Way You Are

**And because you are children, God has sent the Spirit of
his Son into our hearts, crying, "Abba! Father!"**
—Galatians 4:6

A good friend of mine tells her story of being a young mother
with two toddlers. She rarely had time to herself in those days. She
frequently doubted whether she was being a good mother, and this
pressured her to be the "perfect" mother to her small children.
During those years, my friend's self-esteem took quite a battering.
But every afternoon she would turn on the television so her kids
could watch *Mr. Rogers' Neighborhood.* My friend says that the program was the high point of her whole day. She couldn't wait to hear
Mr. Rogers say, "I like you just the way you are."

Being unemployed is a little like being the young mother of small
children. We often wonder whether we are doing enough to find
another job or care for our families. How often do we pressure ourselves to be perfect during an interview? And when we don't get the
job offer or turn up enough new leads or care for our families the way
we think we should, our self-esteem usually suffers.

God, Abba, doesn't demand perfection. As children of God,
we are freed from a slave driver who tells us we aren't doing enough
and aren't good enough. In Christ, God has made us heirs to the
kingdom. God likes us just the way we are. All of us need people to
give voice to God's love, people who like us regardless of our
performance. All of us are children of a God who loves us just the
way we are.

I am a child of God. Abba, I rest in your care.

Intrinsic Worth

And if you belong to Christ, then you are Abraham's offspring, heirs according to the promise.
—Galatians 3:29

The more we identified ourselves with our work in the past, the more abandoned and lost we feel now without a job. When we are living between jobs, we must learn to value ourselves apart from any job.

We are intrinsically worthy simply because we belong to Christ. We are worthy of respect and dignity because each of us lays claim to being "Abraham's offspring, heirs according to the promise." Being heirs to the divine promise is not a position earned by something we do, such as holding down a certain kind of job. Rather, it is a holy gift from God. Knowing this, our self-esteem is unassailable by crisis, misfortune, or unemployment, because its self-worth is tenderly held in the hands of a loving Christ.

It is important that we practice valuing ourselves apart from any job. Sometimes I feel ashamed to be out of work or find I'm giving myself negative messages. But if I stop and remember that I belong to Christ. I become less miserable and feel more worthy. The simple act of pausing to remember who you are as Christ's own will give you strength and empowerment, and self-esteem will return.

I am worthy of self-respect and I have dignity
because I belong to Christ.

Lives Worthy of the Lord

**. . . lead lives worthy of the Lord, fully pleasing
to him, as you bear fruit in every good work and as you
grow in the knowledge of God.
—Colossians 1:10**

It is possible to experience living between jobs as a time of new beginnings and spiritual growth when we continue to "lead lives worthy of the Lord." We please God when we "bear fruit" in works of love that God calls us to do. We grow in the knowledge of God when our lives are rooted in the love of God and his creation.

All of us, at one time or another, have met people who lead lives worthy of God. Even when they go through difficult times, they never think only of themselves. They are convinced of their inherent worth as human beings—as children of God. In response to God's love to them, they reach out and give love to others. They "bear fruit in every good work." They show their gratitude by looking past their own difficulties and helping others. And they become happier people, more satisfied with their own contributions and worth.

We, too, will feel better when we stop worrying only about ourselves and spend some time doing things constructive for others. Obviously we can't abandon our search for satisfying employment, but we have opportunities every day to put God's love into action. Some of the seemingly small acts of love we do for others will brighten their whole day. Their self-esteem may grow as a result of something we say or do—something that proves God's love to them. We know our self-esteem grows when we spend time regularly with people who love and affirm us. God calls us to go beyond *taking*—accepting his affirmation through our loved ones, to *giving*—sharing acts of love with others.

Potential employers will sense our spirit of helpfulness and consideration toward others. They will usually prefer people who work well in a team setting. Sometimes this quality may mean more to them than our experience, skills, and other abilities. They may be looking for that extra something—the something that comes naturally to us when we "lead lives worthy of the Lord."

*Because I am loved by God, I can lead a life worthy of the Lord by
treating myself and others with respect and dignity today.*

Daily Bread

Give us this day our daily bread.
—Matthew 6:11

Unemployment is one of those life crises which strips us to our essentials. In other words, we suddenly stop taking things for granted—a roof over our heads, a regular paycheck, our families, our daily bread. We quickly come to see those life essentials as incredibly precious gifts. We do not own them.

Unemployment radically alters our understanding of ownership. When we own something, we control it, we alone decide what to do with it. Unemployment shows us how little we are in control of the universe and how much life's necessities are gifts from God, not things to possess. How liberating! We are relieved of the burden of ownership, free to experience our families and life's necessities as God's gift of daily bread.

Once I began to see loved ones and life essentials as gifts, I discovered that my very life is a gift of God. I came to see that I'd better appreciate myself, take care of myself, and treat myself with respect and dignity. The gift of life comes with responsibility, and I realized only I could be a responsible steward of this, the most precious of God's gifts. For me, this means doing the best I can to love and appreciate others, knowing I don't control them. I may be able to shape and make the best of my present circumstances, but I do not control them either. I keep up an active job search, remembering all the time that employment is a part of my daily bread, one of life's essentials that will always remain a gift, not something I can ever own.

Stand in awe of God's gifts that sustain you physically and emotionally—and hold lightly to those things and people you can never really control.

Father, Give me this day my daily bread,
gifts of all I need for life and love.

Seeking Support

Turn to me and be gracious to me,
for I am lonely and afflicted.
—Psalm 25:16

Looking for a job can be a lonely experience. Sometimes it feels like it's just "us against the world." But it isn't. God walks beside us and leads us to seek support from others who are also unemployed. I joined a group of such people. We offer each other moral support as well as leads on job openings and personal contacts in various businesses.

There are many, many unemployed people these days. Because we don't compete for exactly the same jobs, we stand to gain emotional support and networking tips by banding together. Many communities, placement services, and state employment development offices have support groups for unemployed people. The goal for many of these groups is often to provide help until everyone in the group is employed again.

Family and friends are also wonderful, vital sources of support during unemployment—no one can take their place as wellsprings of love and encouragement. Still, nobody really experiences unemployment in quite the same way as another job seeker. If you're not already a part of a support group for unemployed people, consider joining one. It will strengthen your base of emotional support while offering valuable networking assistance. It will also make unemployment and job seeking a lot less lonely.

Turn to me, O God, and be gracious to me, for I
am lonely and afflicted. Today, let me meet people who
can support me and whose support I can return.

Faithful Love

**There is no fear in love, but perfect love casts out fear;
for fear has to do with punishment, and whoever
fears has not reached perfection in love.
—1 John 4:18**

When I was new to the Christian faith, I used to think that Christianity was a lot like having a job—if I worked hard and believed hard I would grow spiritually, I could somehow arrive, succeed, finish. After a while I would attain a distinguished level of Christian maturity or at least a kind of benevolent enlightenment.

Unemployment taught me that faith is nothing like having a job; faith is love, not accomplishments or work. Faith is a never-ending experience of growing in Christ. I used to define myself and measure my growth by what I did for a living. Success at living was loosely defined by how well I succeeded at work. When I lost my job, I finally came face-to-face with Jesus alone. I stood before God without the armor of a career to define me.

Faith is living in love one day at a time without fear. Without the distraction of job or career track, we stand before God clothed in Christ's love alone—a love not measured by success, a love that has no end. God's love is not *successful*; God's love is *faithful*, and we have no reason to fear.

*I stand before God alone today, knowing I am
covered in the love of Christ.*

True Happiness

**Happy is everyone who fears the Lord,
who walks in his ways.
—Psalm 128:1**

The Psalms repeatedly define happiness as the fear of God and following God's ways. We may be unemployed, but happiness is within our grasp when we choose to follow the ways of God and grow into the image of Christ. During unemployment we periodically take an inventory of our lives under the eye of God to find out what is working in our lives so that we can discard that which is no longer helpful; we explore our hearts to discover what we really want to do with our lives and what we want out of life; we forgive and seek forgiveness in our relationships. We find that happiness comes when we dare to examine our hearts and relationships, and grow in the ways of God.

And there are other avenues of happiness and growth. Happiness and genuine growth take root when we stay in the present moment God gives us and look for today's blessings rather than catapult ourselves into a future we really don't control. Those blessings are the seeds of growth, for when we let God's blessings into our lives, they take root and produce the energy we need to cope with unemployment. Who can look into the eyes of a loved one, walk on a wave-tossed beach, or receive a warm letter from a friend and say they have *not* grown? These blessings are the stuff of a kind of happiness that can sustain us through set-backs, troubles, and trials.

We know that growth is not simple progress. Journeying the ways of God often seems fraught with detours and switch-backs. But we know it is God in Christ who accompanies us on our journey. And that knowledge, along with the blessings we collect along the way, is genuine happiness. The path twists and turns, the road leads us over peaks and through valleys and we grow.

*I may not have a job at the moment, but I am following
God's ways and growing—and I am happy.*

High Hopes

Why are you cast down within me, O my soul, and why are you disquieted within me? Hope in God; for I shall again praise him, my help and my God.
—Psalm 42:5-6

Mark Twain once said, "Put all your eggs in one basket—and watch that basket." When I interview for a job I really want, well-meaning family members and friends caution me, "Don't put all your eggs in one basket." In other words, don't get your hopes up too much over this one interview; don't get so emotionally involved because you'll only get hurt if things don't work out. But every time I interview for an important job, I do put all my emotional eggs in that one basket. I believe there is nothing wrong with hope—lots of it—even though all I have is one interview, one "basket." I aim high. I have great aspirations. Sure, there may be some pain should I not get the job, but having hope and caring deeply about the work I want to do far outweighs any pain that comes from aiming too high.

During unemployment it is vital that we hope too much. Though the psalmist went through a time of difficult struggle, he had huge hopes in God. At the heart of Christ's gospel are large, wild quantities of hope. After all, we've bet our very lives on God's faithfulness and Christ's grace. And hope in God will sustain us through this chronic crisis of unemployment. So it's okay to put all your eggs in one basket—and watch that basket like a hawk.

Hope in God; for I shall again praise him,
my help and my God.

Aspirations

**O my strength, I will sing praises to you, for you, O God,
are my fortress, the God who shows me steadfast love.
—Psalm 59:17**

God gives us our aspirations. They are gifts of God's steadfast love to keep us strong during unemployment. It is our aspirations that give us the strength and hope to go on.

Living between jobs has uncovered aspirations that I didn't know I had while I was busy working full-time. I not only aspire to a job in my chosen career, but I find I have an even stronger aspiration regarding home and hearth—I have a very strong desire to own my own home. My aspiration to home ownership is a gift from God that gives me the strength and hope to continue the difficult task of seeking employment.

We can all use the time of unemployment to discover hidden aspirations. What strong desire to achieve something high or great is hidden in your heart? Is it centered on job and career? Or are there other, stronger aspirations waiting? You don't have to tell anybody else about our aspirations. You can soar as high as you like in the privacy of your own heart. Nurture those aspirations—they are fuel for hope.

*Today I let my aspirations ascend to God,
my fortress and my strength.*

Dreams and Visions

**Then afterward, I will pour out my spirit on all flesh;
your sons and daughters shall prophesy, your old men shall
dream dreams, and your young men shall see visions.**
—Joel 2:28

I read an article recently about a woman who lives her dreams. Well over seventy, she lives alone on a farm in rural New England. She supports herself as a graphic designer and illustrator of children's books. She also raises various livestock and cultivates a garden. This elderly woman lives exactly the way she dreams. Her home is lit solely by candle light, and she clothes herself in nineteenth-century dress.

We may or may not envy such eccentric dreams. But the gift of the Holy Spirit during unemployment is the time to "dream dreams" and "see visions." If we choose, we can reimagine ourselves in a new work environment or dream ourselves into a new lifestyle. We are limited only by our vision.

Our dreams for our lives and those we love empower us during unemployment. This power comes from the Holy Spirit. When we let ourselves dream dreams and see visions, we build self-esteem and renew our confidence. Dreaming dreams and seeing visions helps us learn what we really want out of life.

Today I accept the Holy Spirit's gift of
dreams and visions for my life.

Appreciating the Ordinary

So all the generations from Abraham to David are fourteen generations, and from David to the deportation to Babylon, fourteen generations; and from the deportation of Babylon to the Messiah, fourteen generations.
—Matthew 1:17

It has been said that God is in the details. Usually, I skip reading biblical genealogies to get on with the real part of the story. But in the Bible, new ideas often begin with a genealogy. It is in the minutia of the centuries that form Jesus' genealogy that God reveals the Christ. God combines generations of seemingly chance encounters and insignificant events to bring forth the salvation of the world.

Often it is the minutia of life—the small, seemingly unimportant events and encounters of everyday life—that are clues to God at work in our lives. God showers us daily with blessings that appear unimportant or ordinary. Through unemployment, God offers us the opportunity to appreciate and savor the details of our lives.

I recently met an unemployed man who was married to a busy professional woman. Because of his new, flexible schedule, he was suddenly able to take a far more active role in raising his two school-age children. He told me that the time he spends simply taking the children to and from school and supervising their after-school activities has reacquainted him with his kids. "It took being unemployed to rediscover what wonderful children we have," he said. "I found that my kids lead such interesting lives, and now I'm more a part of their lives."

Appreciating and savoring the details of daily living enables us to experience God at work in our lives. New joy and new peace await, in the hidden ordinary, the seemingly unimportant encounters and events which make up our days.

I appreciate how ordinary today is by seeking the hidden ways in which God is at work in my life. Today I celebrate the details.

Winter Time

At that time the festival of the Dedication took place
in Jerusalem. It was winter.
—John 10:22

It was winter. It was winter in Jesus' ministry—his doubters had heightened criticism of Jesus and claimed he was possessed of a demon blasphemer. As in most circumstances with which life confronts us, we have a choice about how we view unemployment. We can view it as a long, hard winter—a storm with no end. Or, knowing that winter also passes, we can see unemployment as temporary as the ever-changing seasons.

God's beauty all around us helps us focus on the seasonality of our unemployment. Enter with Jesus into the peaceful, beautiful eye of the storm. Spend some time each day looking for signs of spring in a blade of grass, in a bud on a tree, or in the movements of the sun and stars. Our world is also made beautiful by those we love. Look for the God's beauty in the smile of your child, the way your cat purrs when you hold her, the touch of a dear friend's hand.

God put beauty in the world to call us out of ourselves and our negative fantasies of finality. God calls us into an ever-changing world filled with precious days to be savored and cherished.

Today I look for beauty in the natural world
and in the faces of those I love.

Considering the Lilies

**Consider the lilies, how they grow: they never toil nor spin;
yet I tell you, even Solomon in all his glory was not
clothed like one of these.
—Luke 12:27**

I enjoy having friends to dinner. When friends ask what they can bring to the meal, I usually tell them to bring flowers. During unemployment, beautiful flowers make me feel special. Flowers are one of the many little extras, generally outside my budget, that make life worth living.

"Consider the lilies," Jesus said. Even King Solomon was not dressed as richly as a lily. Yet they never "toil nor spin." They simply *are.* They're one of God's many wonderful creations. Identify those beautiful things that help make life good and regularly treat yourself to them during your unemployment. Beauty doesn't have to cost anything. You can see great art in museums, read good books from libraries, smell fragrant roses in gardens, and watch children playing in city parks—all free of charge. Unemployment allows us a certain flexibility in our schedules. Arrange your weekly schedule to include time for considering the lilies and feeling good.

Today I consider the lilies and look for beauty in this world.

Just to Live

**Consider the ravens: they neither sow nor reap, they
have neither storehouse or barn, and yet God feeds them.
Of how much more value are you than the birds!
—Luke 12:24**

American culture doesn't value "the ravens," those who rely on
the providence of God. Our society only values people who are busy
making a living. Our culture rewards us for dedicating our lives to
our careers, and it especially rewards those who over-achieve by
giving 120 percent to the job.

Society does not value living for its own sake. Yet it is important
to reflect on our lives and on what living means to us, for how we
feel about life will have a significant impact on our choice of career.
It is important that we do not become so obsessed with living only
to work that we forget it is possible to work in order to live.

A friend of mine forever changed the way I viewed work. I had
allowed my work to define me, and everything I held dear was
found only in the office—all of my relationships, even my self-
worth. I lived only to work. However, my friend mastered the art of
holding work lightly. He viewed work as a human activity that
enhanced his life and relationships, but he understood his life to be
a holy gift, something to be enjoyed and explored fully. Unlike me,
my friend worked in order to live.

Rabbi Abraham Heschel spoke for the ravens when he said,
"Just to be is a blessing. Just to live is holy." Life is a gift from a good
and loving God who values us only for ourselves. Therefore, simply
living is holy work—it is worship. Our careers should enhance the
holiness of our lives. Try spending five minutes today sitting quietly
and reverently. Concentrate on your life. Take deep, even breaths.
With each breath, thank God for the sacredness of your existence.

Today I am a raven.

Becoming

For I think that God has exhibited us apostles as last of all,
as though sentenced to death, because we have become
a spectacle to the world, to angels and to mortals.
—1 Corinthians 4:9

The price of apostleship was high in the early centuries of Christianity. It involved becoming "a spectacle to the world, to angels and to mortals." Being an apostle often felt like a death sentence for Christ's sake.

Unemployment also carries a high price to become the people we are. Yet the experience can become a crucible of spiritual growth, helping us become more like Christ. We all remember better times when life was easier and things were going well. But good times alone do little to build character and bring out the best in us. Those things that make human beings excellent (including faith, strength, pride, courage, and hope) are developed and honed by the daily challenges that come with unemployment. When we find the energy to keep job searching and minimize anxiety, we rise to the occasion. We find new, untapped inner resources of strength, pride, courage and hope. And when we have "one of *those* days" when our new-found inner resources seem to fail, we have the privilege and joy of turning to God, family members, and friends for support and care.

Just as paying the price to be an apostle shaped Paul into the image of Christ, our challenges and struggles teach us the value of living, really living each day to the fullest under God. Our days take on new, deeper meaning.

It may cost us something to become apostles. We are becoming human beings appreciating anew the value of home, family, friends, and faith. We are becoming human beings of depth and spirit who are learning that life is too precious and too holy to be taken for granted.

Today, I make my way toward becoming who I am in Christ.
I am strong, proud, courageous and hopeful, and
I take nothing and no one for granted.

The Good Fight

**Fight the good fight of faith; take hold of the eternal life
to which you were called when you made the good confes-
sion in the presence of many witnesses.**
—1 Timothy 6:12

When I first lost my job, I wondered what other people would
think when I told them I was unemployed. I imagined that, upon
first hearing the news, my family and friends would think less of me.
Consequently, I spent those first couple of months ashamed of
myself for losing my job. Initially, I spent so much time being
ashamed that it took me a while to hear and accept the support and
love of family and friends.

"Reputation," Thomas Paine wrote, "is what men and women
think of us; character is what God and the angels know of us." As
I began to look at character differently, I realized that people who
really loved me, loved me for my true self—my character. My
reputation applied to the general public, those associates and
acquaintances who may very well have thought less of me. I'd
be lying if I said I didn't mind how my reputation was weathering
during my unemployment. I cared very much. But gradually I
learned to let go of my earthly reputation and fight the good fight,
taking hold of the eternal life to which God calls me.

With the help of loved ones I began to see that God is more
interested in my character than my reputation. God gives me faith,
courage, strength, hope, love, and gentleness—these are what it
takes to fight the good fight. God helps us survive unemployment
by forming our characters. And character is what matters most.
Reputation will take care of itself.

With God's help and the character God forms in me,
I can fight the good fight today.

Character Building

*. . . we boast in our sufferings, knowing that suffering
produces endurance, and endurance produces character, and
character produces hope, and hope does not disappoint us,
because God's love has been poured into our hearts
through the Holy Spirit that has been given to us.*
—**Romans 5:3-5**

I am a natural-born pessimist. If there is a dark cloud to a silver lining, I'll find it. For me, living between jobs feels too much like a bad dream come true. True to type, I too easily believe that unemployment is all bad. Well, it's not exactly fun. But I can let the experience of unemployment give me endurance, which produces character, which in turn produces hope.

Our character can help us survive unemployment. If I continually allow the pessimistic aspect of my character to react negatively to the challenges unemployment brings, that pessimism will be subtly communicated to potential employers. In planning my next interview, I can cultivate a sense of eagerness and anticipation, a sense of hope in God, who does not disappoint.

I have slowly learned to comport myself with dignity and self-esteem because the Holy Spirit has poured God's love into my heart. I also feel better when I show the world that I am proud of myself and my efforts to find employment. I no longer let my natural pessimism cloud my vision. My family, friends, and associates respond positively to this new me. Hoping in God's love builds character—the character needed to endure the hardships of unemployment.

*Today I am a person of character. I endure unemployment's
hardships by believing in the love of God.*

Dreaming with Angels

And he dreamed that there was a ladder set up on the earth, and the top of it reached to heaven; and behold, the angels of God were ascending and descending on it.
—Genesis 28:12

Unemployment offers us the time and opportunity to dream. But sometimes we censor the dreams we have for our own lives. My current fantasy is to become a full-time writer and support myself while working out of a cottage in the country. When I daydream about my writing career, I can just see the cottage and its garden, I know the room in which I will write, I can feel the shape of my days. Then I tell myself, "Don't be so silly. That dream will never come true." Or "How can you be so childish? Unemployment is very serious—you better stop dreaming and start coping."

God's angels descend and ascend in our dreams. It doesn't matter whether the dreams actually "come true." What matters is that dreams open our minds and hearts to ways in which God may be leading us into a new life. Dreaming and fantasizing give us important information about those things we value in life, how we experience the Christian faith, and how we want to grow spiritually. Our dreams identify and honor the people God has created us to be. Our dreams help us aim high and increase the possibility of getting what we want out of life. Our dreams improve our relationship with God.

I may never be able to make enough money as a full-time writer to support a life in a country cottage. But my dream taught me that writing is important to me and that it is one way God speaks to me. Now I can begin to seek employment that allows energy and time for writing in my spare time. My dream offers me a little bit of heaven to cope with unemployment in a creative way.

It may be that not all of our dreams come true, but that's no reason to censor them. Our dreams are stairways to heaven.

Today I dream with the angels.

Impossible Dreams

A man was there named Zacchaeus; he was a chief tax
collector and was rich. He was trying to see who Jesus was,
but on account of the crowd he could not, because
he was short of stature. So he ran on ahead and
climbed up into a sycamore tree to see him,
because he was to pass that way.
—Luke 19:2-4

Zacchaeus had a dream—he wanted to see who Jesus was. Zacchaeus had two strikes against him: Because he was a tax collector and tax collectors were thought to cheat people, Zacchaeus was regarded as a sinner, and therefore spiritually unable to approach a holy man; his short height also prevented him from seeing Jesus. And yet he did not let the impossible stand in the way of realizing his dream. Zacchaeus took a playful approach to seeing Jesus— he climbed a tree.

During unemployment, it is critical to our well-being that we playfully encourage dreams of a better life for ourselves and our relationship with God. Playful dreaming helps us cope with difficult times. It encourages a positive attitude and shows us all kinds of possibilities for a new life in spite of our circumstances.

We do ourselves a disservice when we try to tame our dreams, dismiss them as impossible, or conform them to the real world. Zacchaeus didn't let the real world interfere with his dream of seeing Jesus. Rather, he creatively found a way to make his dream come true. We each have a Zacchaeus in us who encourages us to dream the impossible. Wild and "impossible" dreams encourage new ways to grow in Christ and develop a positive outlook during unemployment. Such playful imagining and dreaming can also help us find creative ways to make our dreams come true. Let's not be afraid to climb a tree today. It may make a dream come true

Today I let God guide me toward my dreams.

Interpreting Our Lives

**They said to him, "We have had dreams, and there is no
one to interpret them." And Joseph said to them, "Do not
interpretations belong to God? Please tell them to me."
—Genesis 40:8**

Unemployment is a time to interpret our lives under the eye of
God. It is a time of sorting ourselves out. While we are living
between jobs, we can interpret our lives and dreams, like Joseph, and
as a result maybe decide to do some things differently. We can ask
ourselves the questions "In what areas of my life is God calling me to
change?", "What relationships do I need to repair or rebuild?", and
"Are there feelings, relationships or attitudes that I need to let
go of?" And we can ask God to help us interpret the answers.

Interpreting our lives also means identifying those areas in which
dreams can come true. It is important to our well-being that we
identify how our dreams find their way into our daily lives. When
we know we have realized some of our dreams, we know it's possible
to realize other dreams in the future. So we ask ourselves questions
like, "Where in my life, right now, have my dreams come true?",
"Which relationships are strong and healthy?", "What signs do I
have that God is loving and caring for me today?", and "What good
things am I doing now to make my other dreams come true?"

Follow Joseph's example. Question your life and dreams, and
identify how you can live your dreams daily.

Today I interpret my life and dreams under the eye of God.

Opportunities

**So the two of them went on until they came to Bethlehem.
When they came to Bethlehem, the whole town
was stirred because of them; and the
women said, "Is this Naomi?"
—Ruth 1:19**

"God helps those who help themselves" may not be a verse from the Bible, but that old saying sure seems to sum up the story of Naomi. Out of adversity, Naomi made an opportunity for herself and her daughter-in-law Ruth. The trip to Bethlehem and a chance for a new life must have been hard on Naomi and Ruth. But Naomi had a plan to survive.

Although bad things like unemployment do indeed happen to good people, we can transform negative experiences into opportunities. We can passively wait around for good luck to find us, or we can actively seek out and seize whatever opportunities each new day offers.

I have an unemployed friend who needed to find a new job as quickly as possible. But she also had other goals concerning her personal growth and relationships. Not satisfied with the progress she was making in California toward either goal, my friend decided to make her own opportunity in Washington state. She had a plan to survive there and the determination to follow it through. Six weeks after moving to Washington, my friend found employment and relationships she couldn't find in California.

The moral to this story, as that of the book of Ruth, is to search faithfully for opportunities for a better life and, when necessary, create them yourself under the eye of God.

*Today is filled with opportunities for a better life. I greet
the day ready to seize the opportunities God provides for me
or create new opportunities with God's support.*

Living Sacrifice

**I appeal to you therefore, brothers and sisters, by the
mercies of God, to present your bodies as a living sacrifice,
holy and acceptable to God, which is
your spiritual worship.
—Romans 12:1**

Yogi Berra, a master of the malapropism, once said, "Baseball
is 90 percent mental. The other half is physical." This applies to
unemployment as well. The "mental" is keeping a positive attitude
in spite of our circumstances. It's not only critical to finding a new
job, but it's also a kind of spiritual worship. Maintaining a positive
mental outlook reinforces our spiritual belief that God, rather than
unemployment, is Lord in our lives. A positive mind-set is a type of
worship offering to God. It is a tangible expression of our hope in
God alone.

When we take care of our physical bodies, we offer ourselves as a
living sacrifice to God. Our mental and spiritual outlook continues to
improve. We need plenty of exercise and rest in order to cope with
unemployment. We need to schedule time each day to nurture our
spirits in prayer, and reenergize our bodies in activity and rest.

Life is too precious, even during the difficult times of unemployment, to waste it. Nurturing good thoughts during unemployment
nourishes our bodies and our souls. Spiritual worship assures us that
we are holy people and acceptable to God, now and forever.

*There is time today for prayer, exercise, rest, and keeping a positive
outlook. There is time today for spiritual worship.*

A New Thing

**I am about to do a new thing; now it springs forth,
do you not perceive it? I will make a way in the
wilderness and rivers in the desert.
—Isaiah 43:19**

An old Yiddish proverb says, "If you've got nothing to lose, you can try everything." When we consider making a major job or career change, we have the opportunity "to do a new thing," almost to reinvent ourselves. When we feel trapped in our work, we dream about who we would like to be in our next job and how we could present ourselves differently to the world.

A friend of mine once had a job where it was acceptable for him to keep his hair long and wear jeans to work. His colleagues always viewed him as a kid just out of school who had risen as high as he could in the organization. My friend felt trapped by the perceptions of his colleagues and he decided he wanted to reinvent himself by adopting a corporate image and finding different work. He cut his hair, bought a three-piece suit, and looked for a different job. Many years later, he told me how much fun he had by completely changing his style and image.

While in transition from one career to another, it is fun to dream and experiment with a variety of styles of dress and ways of relating with others. Doing a brand new thing in our lives opens us up to God. Imagine how you would like to dress for work everyday. Then imagine the kind of relationships you would like to develop with new people. Imagine various jobs or careers that would allow you to develop different parts of your personality and interests. In other words, reinvent yourself today. Remember, "If you've got nothing to lose, you can try everything."

*Today I will use my imagination to see how God
might be doing a new thing in my life.*

Life-Changing Experience

Did you experience so much for nothing?
—if it really was for nothing.
—Galatians 3:4

The Galatians were too eager to exchange their experience of Christ's gospel of grace for a gospel of the works of the law. To paraphrase an exasperated Paul writing to the Galatians, "Was your experience of grace all for nothing; could it not sustain you during a time when you were tempted to follow after a false gospel of works?"

It's been said that experience is a valuable teacher. It is a teacher the Galatians chose to ignore—at their peril. However, unemployment offers us plenty of valuable experiences that can sustain us until we find a job. Unemployment offers valuable professional experience. I have found it has developed my networking skills, increased my ability to recognize and act on opportunity, and definitely improved my verbal and written communication skills.

Unemployment also offers valuable personal experience. I was recently having coffee with a friend who is also unemployed. Unemployment, she said, has forced her to be more flexible in how she approaches unplanned job opportunities or how she reacts to sudden rejection. She told me that her husband noticed her new flexibility toward life and that he is definitely happy with the change.

Unemployment is a time when we are actively acquiring new professional and personal experiences. We can, if we choose, take time to reflect on the kind of experience that will make us better employees and human beings. Friends and family members are great resources in helping us identify the kind of experience we are getting. I try regularly to ask trusted loved ones about how I'm different now that I'm unemployed. The feedback is almost always positive and it makes me feel good. My prayer life and general attitude toward God has changed for the better as well. Each day that I am unemployed and yet survive is a day of thanksgiving for me. We may be looking for work daily, but we are also gaining precious life-changing experience.

Experience is what I'm getting while looking for work.
All experience—professional, personal, and spiritual—is valuable
when I pay attention to what I'm learning.

Goodness of God

Jesus said to him, "Why do you call me good?
No one is good but God alone."
—Luke 18:19

Faith is believing in and experiencing the goodness of God in Jesus Christ. We need to believe in the goodness of God more than ever during unemployment. Believing that there is a power of goodness at work in our lives liberates us to enjoy the present and look forward to the future. Experiencing God's goodness is surrendering each day into Jesus' hands, trusting that every encounter, each situation, and every moment is in some way good for us.

Signs of God's goodness can be large and easy to see, like finally getting the job you've worked hard to get. But most often signs of God's goodness at work in our lives are small, hidden in the moments of our daily lives. We must pay attention to our lives and look for them as well.

Recently I experienced a dry period in my job search—no new leads on jobs, nothing appropriate in job listings suited to my skills, no interviews at all. In other words, the large, clear signs of the goodness of God at work were absent. But one evening during this dry spell I was reading in bed when my cat jumped up, snuggled up next to me purring deeply, and went to sleep. As I stroked his fur and listened to his contented purring, I thought what an incredible, beautiful blessing it was to have this cat during this time in my life. I was overwhelmed by the goodness of God made real in the presence of my cat. It was a small, but critically important sign to me that God was still at work for good in my life.

Hold fast to the visible and invisible goodness of God. We can enjoy elements of our present circumstances and look forward to tomorrow, trusting that God is at work for good in our lives.

God is at work for good in my life today. I will look for signs,
large and small, of goodness.

Family and Friends

**Some friends play at friendship but a true friend
sticks closer than one's nearest kin.
—Proverbs 18:24**

The support of our families is extremely important to us during unemployment. Their love and care help give us the motivation and energy we need to thrive and keep an active job search. For some of us, families are able to help us out financially until we can secure employment. For others, simply the love of family is enough.

However, sometimes our families are just too close to us and worry too much about us. They put pressure on us and give lots of advice at a time when we need simple understanding instead.

We cannot ask our families to bear the full stress and strain of our unemployed circumstances. Now more than ever, we must cultivate and nurture our friendships. Friends are people who love us at a healthy distance. Paradoxically, friends are especially helpful because they're not as close as family. In other words, friends love us and offer care and support without the emotional history that creates family ties. Friends love us for who we are but go on about their business pursuing their own lives, loves, and work apart from us. For example, I find it wonderful to meet a friend and listen to developments in her life that are very different from my own. It keeps me from dwelling on my own problems concerning my family or unemployment.

Families are wonderful gifts. We cannot survive and thrive during unemployment without their love and support. Friends love and support us in a different, complimentary way and are just as critical to our growth during unemployment. We can thank God for the care of both family and friends in our lives.

*I thank God for true friends who love and
support me from a distance.*

Nurturing Friendships

**. . . but I have called you friends, because I have made
known to you everything that I have heard from my Father.
—John 15:15**

Nurturing old friendships and making new friends is absolutely critical to surviving unemployment. As Jesus journeyed toward his death and resurrection, he needed friends, not only servants or disciples. Just as friendship sustained Jesus during the critical end of his earthly ministry, friendship can sustain us during the crisis of unemployment. We must take time away from job searches and family demands to connect with friends.

I decided the best way for me to schedule time with friends was to buy a special social calendar. I bought a beautifully designed desk calendar with gorgeous pictures of the French countryside on which to record my social engagements. On this calendar, I recorded only dates and times spent with friends. Job interviews or engagements with family are recorded on calendars of their own. My social calendar is a friendship diary that shows me how blessed I am with friends.

I find that regularly scheduling time to be with friends is a real boost to my self-esteem. Talking with friends about their own work, lives and loves takes our minds off our own problems. And offering friends simple hospitality, even on a budget tightened by unemployment, is wonderfully empowering. Looking back through the past couple of months on my social calendar, I see I spent time with friends during walks in the park behind my house, on video-viewing nights, and while sharing sunsets from my deck.

Such times with friends are not only diverting and entertaining, they also remind us that there is more to life than the chronic crisis of unemployment. Life is a gift of God. And developing and nurturing friendships is one of the best ways to enjoy the gift of life.

Today I will schedule time to spend with a friend.

Be Gentle

**. . . Show by your good life that your works are done
with gentleness born of wisdom.
—James 3:13**

Often the world is not a gentle place. This is especially true as
we continue to seek employment. Looking for a job means entering
a competitive world in which only the strong survive, a world in
which we are sometimes handled pretty roughly. Gentleness is one
of the hallmarks of the Christian life. Not only are we called by grace
to show gentleness toward others, but we are also called to treat
ourselves gently.

We must be gentle with ourselves internally and externally.
Whenever possible, our self-talk, should consist of hopeful words.
Recently I was frustrated during an interview because I felt like
I wasn't communicating clearly with a potential employer. I left the
interview angry with myself, giving myself all kinds of negative inter-
nal feedback and growing more depressed as I got in the car. On the
drive home, I realized I had beaten myself up enough, and I decided
to take a gentler tone. I began to tell myself I had done the best I
could in a difficult situation and that it takes two to fail to communicate. Not surprisingly, I began to feel better and more hopeful about
my next interview. When I got home, I fixed a special dinner and
invited a friend over for the evening. I finished my day with a long,
luxurious soak in a hot bath.

Making a special occasion out of a disappointing day is a good
way to be gentle with ourselves. If Christ can treat us with gentleness
and care, surely we can imitate him. Such gentleness restores our
spirits. It is balm for bruised psyches and tired bodies. The world
is tough enough on us. We don't need to go out of our way to
be tough on ourselves. Gentleness is the strength we need to see
us through.

*Because I am forgiven by Christ, I can be gentle
toward others and myself today.*

Gracious Living

**But you, O Lord, are a God merciful and gracious,
slow to anger and abounding in steadfast
love and faithfulness.
—Psalm 86:15**

To be gracious while living between jobs means to cultivate a generosity of spirit toward others and ourselves. As God has dealt generously and gracefully with us, we too must deal generously and gracefully with others. Generously opening our homes to others is one way to promote healing, for it protects us from the temptation to isolate ourselves until we find the job we want.

When I get wrapped up in my job search and consumed with anxiety or shame, I invite people to my home for pot-lucks. Sharing a simple meal with them keeps me connected to a world much larger than the anxious world of job-seekers. Entertaining at home enlarges my world and my spirit. After one of these suppers I feel as though my very being has expanded and become more generous.

Being gracious toward ourselves is treating ourselves with lavish, tender care. We try to eliminate negative self-talk—getting down on ourselves. Instead, we surround ourselves with people who love and support us. We focus on our gifts and skills and find ways to use them; we treat ourselves to things we really enjoy—attending a concert or sports event, driving through the countryside, or whatever it takes. Our God is a gracious, welcoming God, whose very Spirit generously expands our lives—even while living between jobs.

*Because God is gracious with me, I am gracious toward
those I meet today and toward myself.*

Healing Wounds

**He himself bore our sins in his body on the cross, so that,
free from sins, we might live for righteousness; by his
wounds you have been healed.**
—1 Peter 2:24

Unemployment is a significant wounding. We have been hurt by the loss of our jobs, by rejections from potential employers, and by the harsh reality of finite financial resources. But the wounds we receive from unemployment can be healed by the One wounded on the cross. Our wounds can deepen our faith and expand our capacity for love.

We follow Christ, the Wounded Healer. Because Jesus was wounded for our sake, we can face and accept the pain that comes from being unemployed. Often admitting and accepting the pain requires a trusted friend in whom we can honestly confide, a therapist, or a small group of people going through experiences similar to ours. Jesus can heal us through the love and support of our communities.

After we've confronted and embraced the pain, we can then let go of it—let it go to a place inside us where Jesus offers resurrection and new life. There, with Jesus, the Lover of our wounded souls, we'll find our wounds have made us better lovers of God and others. We'll find we naturally want to help and support those who've been wounded as we have. By his wounds we are healed.

*Unemployment has wounded me. Today Jesus helps me accept
the pain and move on toward resurrection.*

Healthy and Well

**Beloved, I pray that all may go well with you
and that you may be in good health,
just as it is well with your soul.
—3 John 2**

There is a lot of truth in the old saying, "When you've got your health, you've got everything." Unemployment often points out those things that are now absent from our lives—a job, extra money, peace of mind, and possibly health insurance, for example. Yet health is one part of our lives we usually take for granted, no matter what our circumstances. But to under-appreciate our health during unemployment robs us of a great blessing and a veritable wellspring of happiness. The writer of 3 John equates good health with the wellness of the soul. Taking time to appreciate good health will remind us that our lives are not empty, that there is a source of abundance even during unemployment.

Staying healthy is critical to surviving and thriving during unemployment. Staying healthy means paying attention to our bodies by eating a well-balanced diet and getting plenty of exercise.

It's obvious we need our health to cope with the stress of a competitive job search. But maintaining good health is also a way to keep our souls well; good health helps us enjoy our relationship with God. It promotes not only physical but also spiritual well-being. A regular exercise program and a good diet strengthens our bodies to cope with the stress that comes with unemployment. Now that we are between jobs, we can schedule time to take a brisk walk regularly, and to prepare tasty, well-balanced meals.

A good deal of happiness lies in health. During unemployment we need all the happiness we can get! Caring for our bodies makes for happiness—and a well-cared-for soul.

*I do not take my health for granted. Today, I have time
to take care of myself, to exercise and eat well,
and to enjoy the Lord my God.*

Restore Me to Health

**O Lord, by these things people live, and in all these
is the life of my spirit. Oh, restore me to
health and make me live!**
—Isaiah 38:16

I had my hair cut yesterday and told the hairdresser that with my hair so short I can see more gray hair now than ever before. She replied, "You've earned each one of those gray hairs." I certainly have. Each gray hair has a story to tell. I decided not to color my hair (at least not yet) because I want to tell the world, and especially potential employers, that I am a woman of experience and maturity.

Our bodies are like walking autobiographies, telling everyone the major and minor stresses of our lives. Maintaining our overall health, including a good diet and grooming, tells the world how successfully we are able to manage stress in our lives. We all know that potential employers often make decisions during interviews based on how healthy and well-groomed we appear. My gray hair is one way my body subtly reinforces the experience demonstrated in my résumé. Unfortunately, I am quite thin and my body may communicate to potential employers that I don't handle stress well. Therefore, I am currently developing a good diet to restore my health and put on a little more weight.

Good health, a balanced diet, and regular exercise reflected in our bodies are also parts of our walking autobiographies, telling the world we feel good about ourselves and are competent professionals who know how to manage stress constructively. Part of our daily routine should be to thank God for good health or to pray for good health when needed. Feeling healthy raises our self-esteem and reduces stress because when we feel good, we have more physical and emotional energy to cope with the challenges unemployment presents.

*I am coping with unemployment and projecting a positive image
during interviews because today I take care of my health.*

God Brought Laughter

Now Sarah said, "God has brought laughter for me; everyone who hears will laugh with me."
—Genesis 21:6

Sarah laughed when God's messenger told her she would have a child long after her child-bearing years were over. All the years of frustration and bitterness over being childless finally boiled over into laughter. The messenger made her a ridiculous promise to end a seemingly hopeless situation. What else could Sarah do but laugh? And when the child was finally born, Sarah laughed again and named her son Isaac, which in Hebrew means "He Laughs".

Being jobless offers plenty of frustration. And we sometimes respond with tears. However, we can also respond with laughter. We can learn from Sarah. Laughter, like tears, is good medicine—it's a wonderful release. We feel somehow stronger after a good laugh.

Laughter is the best medicine when taken in the company of friends. Laughing and having fun with friends gets us out of ourselves, transports us out of isolation and into the joy of companionship. The ability to laugh at ourselves and laugh with others eases the frustration that unemployment can bring. We begin to see that we can enjoy ourselves. And we find in friends the support we need to keep us going.

Laughter releases pent up frustration and gives us a break from the problems of unemployment. It restores the energy we need to get a fresh perspective on our circumstances.

Like Sarah I will laugh at my jobless situation
and at my reaction to it.

Being Silly

Then the Lord opened the mouth of the donkey, and it said to Balaam, "What have I done to you, that you have struck me these three times?" Balaam said to the donkey, "Because you have made a fool of me! I wish I had a sword in my hand! I would kill you right now!"
—Numbers 22:28-29

Balaam was going about his business when his donkey suddenly saw an angel of the Lord standing in the middle of the road. Balaam couldn't see a thing, though, so he beat his donkey to make him continue. God then spoke to Balaam through the mouth of the donkey. It is one of the most humorous moments in scripture.

Looking for work is serious business. We are very earnest about making contacts, writing our résumés, scanning job listings, and pursuing openings whenever we hear of them. We are even careful about our clothes, choosing suits and outfits to make just the right impression on an interview. We never underestimate the importance of preparation during unemployment.

However, we occasionally need a break from all this intensive planning. We need to learn the importance of being silly without feeling foolish. We must give ourselves permission to be very silly from time to time. I was whisked off at nine o'clock one night by a church group to sing "God Bless America" at the top of our lungs beneath one of the largest flags in the United States flying atop one of the county's tallest flagpoles. We made fools of ourselves. People in the neighborhood came out on their porches to laugh at us. It was a very silly thing to do—and we enjoyed ourselves immensely.

God is not offended by our being silly once in a while. Cutting up occasionally during a stressful period in life, like unemployment, does wonders for the soul. I find I'm still earnest about pursuing a new job, but I hold the process a little more lightly.

When earnestness threatens to overwhelm me,
I can do something silly today.

Resting in God

**So then, a sabbath rest still remains
for the people of God.
—Hebrews 4:9**

Activity for activity's sake rarely accomplishes anything, and while unemployed we often put pressure on ourselves or feel pressured from loved ones to be constantly busy. We tell ourselves, "I can't afford to waste a moment until I find a job." Or, "There's so much to do around the house. When I'm not interviewing or sending out résumés, I've got to keep busy here." Or, "I don't want anyone to think I'm lazy." Filling our schedules without any focus or goal except to avoid feeling guilty is neither efficient nor productive.

God knows we need to rest regularly. That's why a sabbath rest is commanded for all of God's people. Sometimes the most productive and faithful thing we can do is nothing at all. Resting and relaxing in God alone not only restores our souls, but it also can allow unconscious desires, dreams, and yearnings to surface into our conscious mind. Two of the big questions during unemployment are, "What do I really want to do in my work and in the next part of my life?" and "What is God calling me to do now?" These questions are the most difficult to answer. Sometimes answers begin to surface while we are doing nothing but taking a sabbath rest in Christ. When our minds are not preoccupied with taking care of business, our deepest dreams and desires reveal themselves to us.

Regularly rest in God. Build rest time into your weekly schedule. An hour spent on a park bench gazing at the flowers or watching children play may be the most productive and faithful way to spend a day. Taking a long, rambling walk or spending an hour in prayer and meditation may be the most efficient way to spend time. Our dreams and desires are elusive things—and sometimes so is God. We must coax them into consciousness with promises of soothing, simple rest.

*Taking a sabbath rest is an important, productive
and faithful part of my work today.*

Surprise!

**But many who are first will be last,
and the last will be first.
—Matthew 19:30**

Imagine life without surprises. How dull and predictable it would be. The element of surprise in life is one of the differences between living fully and merely surviving. Surprise adds spice and excitement, that delightful feeling of not knowing what's going to happen next. Jesus is the master of surprise. His parables are filled with surprise endings, such as the first will be last and the last will be first. These surprise endings completely changed the perspective of his listeners and turned the world on its head.

Trying to control tomorrow by trying to control the actions of others is really an attempt to eliminate surprise from life. I've spent a lot of energy uselessly trying to control tomorrow's outcome. It took becoming unemployed to show me that all my orchestrated actions were really attempts to manipulate God and others into doing what I wanted. They were the desperate actions of a control freak.

Being unemployed has taught me I have little control over events or others—especially God. Ultimately, I can't control job offers or rejections, or even whether my résumé is read or I'm invited to interview because a friend recommended me. All I can really control is remaining faithful to God and being open to whatever surprises Jesus may have in store for me tomorrow. When I let go of the need to control others and events, I enjoy and experience to the fullest whatever surprises God may bring. Giving up control, I no longer fear and instead look forward to tomorrow's surprises.

Unemployment is a crisis in life that shows us how little we are in control. But it also invites us to enjoy life more fully. It opens us up to the unexpected surprises that make faith rich and interesting.

*I look forward to God's surprises today because I am letting
go of my need to control the uncontrollable.*

Giving Love

We love because he first loved us.
—1 John 4:19

When we are between jobs, we need to know that we are loved for who we *are*, not for what we do. We not only need to receive love, we also need to give love.

A friend of mine took a trip to Boston, and before he left his seven year-old son asked his dad to bring something back for him. When my friend got home, his son asked, "Whaddya bring me, Daddy?" His father pulled a small rock out of his pocket and said, "A genuine rock all the way from Boston." I couldn't believe how delighted the child was with the rock. To the little boy, the rock was a way to hold his father's love in his hands. In receiving his father's love, he was on his way to giving love in response.

We may not be employed, but we have a lot to give. Giving love can extend beyond the family to our communities. By volunteering for a community organization a few hours a week or taking up a new ministry at church, we may uncover gifts, skills, or talents we never knew we had. Sometimes such work gives us important information about what kind of job we'd like to have next.

We love because God first loved us. In giving love, God helps us to take the focus off ourselves and our problems in order to love others. When we love others as God loves us, we thrive during unemployment.

I have a lot of love to give today. Let me find
creative ways to express my love.

Wisdom in Love

To get wisdom is to love oneself;
to keep understanding is to prosper.
—Proverbs 19:8

Unemployment is a challenge to self-esteem. We are so used to identifying our self-worth by what we do for a living that we often don't know what we're worth anymore. Yet God's wisdom teaches us to love ourselves for many reasons and in many ways. By turning to someone else, for example, we can see what's worthy about ourselves. And by giving love we can bring out and offer our very best.

Love is work. Loving another person takes skill, creativity, and commitment—attributes we used in our jobs. Whether the object of our love is a spouse or significant other, family member, friend, or community, we can express this love through works as well as words.

A clergywoman I know had just begun work in a small rural parish when she was confronted by an old man in her congregation who was vehemently against women ministers. He went out of his way to tell her to her face that all clergywomen wanted to be men. My friend believed deeply that the church is a community committed to love, so instead of giving up on the man she decided to love him even if it meant he never changed his view of women ministers. Every day my friend baked a pie, cake, or cookies and brought the baked goods to the man's house. She simply chatted with him as if he were a neighbor instead of a parishioner. Slowly, the man came to see her as a good friend instead of as a clergywoman.

My friend didn't do all that baking because it was her job. She did it because love demands wisdom, skill, creativity, and commitment. Love, not the ministry, was her work. And it is ours also. We may be unemployed, but we have work to do—we have love to give.

I have work to do today. I have love to give, using skill, creativity,
and commitment in expressing my love, my self-esteem.

Abundant Love

May mercy, peace, and love be yours in abundance.
—Jude 2

I have a friend who is an environmentalist and naturalist. He's fond of saying, "We are only animals, you know." And that is partly true: we have bodies to feed and clothe and shelter; we have instincts to obey. But we are also human beings. Besides food and shelter, love is perhaps the most important necessity for human life. Giving and accepting love is what makes life worth living. Love feeds our souls. During unemployment, when the basic necessities of food, clothing, and shelter seem more precarious than ever, it is critical to give and accept love in abundance.

Unemployment is a time of crisis and uncertainty. Accepting mercy, peace, and love strengthens us to meet the difficulties we face. God loves us in many different ways throughout the day. There is the love we receive from pets, from our families and friends, from other members of our church, from our neighbors, and even from ourselves.

Let's not be choosy about the manifestations of the love God gives us. Rather, let's constantly be on the lookout for whatever kind of love God offers from moment to moment.

It is often difficult to accept love. We are used to trying to be in control, and it's especially true now as we seek to shorten the length of time we're unemployed. Here are some ways to practice gracefully and gratefully accepting different kinds of love: meditate, go out for coffee with a close friend, take the dog for a long walk, pray, or make a date with your spouse. Whatever the day may bring, know that God loves you abundantly

I accept gracefully and gratefully
God's abundant love today.

Without Money

Ho, everyone who thirsts, come to the waters; and you that have no money, come, buy and eat! Come, buy wine and milk without money and without price.
—Isaiah 55:1

"In God we trust" appears on all of our paper money. Yet we often put more trust in money than God. American culture claims money has the power to make life continue, and to a certain extent that's true. Money keeps a roof over our heads, puts shoes on our feet, and food in the refrigerator. Trusting in God takes a lot of faith when there are bills to be paid with limited financial resources.

Still, as much as we need money to purchase life's basic necessities, money has no real power to bless us with the love and support of family and friends. Money has no power to strengthen our spiritual life or inspire us to grow in love and empathy. Money has no power to create beauty and goodness in ourselves and in the world. Only God has that power and, more importantly, the love to provide us with all of these things.

Trust in God blossoms greatly under adversity, especially under economic adversity. During unemployment money becomes very important, a precious resource to be managed carefully and wisely. But to survive unemployment, we need love and support, patience and strength, inspiration and growth, beauty and goodness. We need the milk of God that has no price. Only the blessings God gives us make life worth living.

Trusting in God's willingness to shower us with blessings puts the power of money in perspective—and we are then a little more free of the anxiety that unemployment brings.

In God I trust. Today I go to God to buy spiritual water,
milk and wine without price.

Other Resources

He sat down opposite the treasury, and watched the
crowd putting money into the treasury. Many rich people
put in large sums. And a poor widow came and put in two
small copper coins, which are worth a penny. Then he called
to his disciples and said to them, "Truly I tell you, this poor
widow has put in more than all those who are contributing
to the treasury. For all of them have contributed out of
their abundance but she out of her poverty has put
in everything she had, all she had to live on."
—Mark 12:41-44

We're unemployed and money is pretty tight. But surviving
unemployment is a matter of attitude, especially when money isn't as
plentiful a resource as it once was. When money is scarce, we need to
remember that we have other resources besides money to live on.
The poor widow's attitude toward money must have been one of
complete trust in the love of God. God was the only resource the
widow had, so she confidently deposited the coins with faith in God,
her provider.

Developing and maintaining a positive attitude in response to
unemployment helps us enjoy life instead of postponing joy until we
have a job again. Attitude is improved and developed by taking
inventory of the resources besides money at our disposal. We must
never overlook our skills, talents, and abilities as resources that enable
us to survive unemployment. Our talents and abilities don't go away
simply because we don't have a job. Using these skills during unemployment improves attitude, builds self-esteem, and restores our
sense of self-worth. Finally, our attitude can reflect our trust in the
love that God has for us now and always. God will take care of us,
as he did the poor widow.

My general attitude is important to surviving unemployment.
I know God has provided me with other resources besides
money to help me live today.

Managing Money

Keep your lives free from the love of money, and be content with what you have; for he has said, "I will never leave you or forsake you."
—Hebrews 13:5

How many times have we heard or recited the old saying, "Money isn't everything"? Unemployed people know, however, that while money may not be *everything*, it sure comes close. For most of us the biggest source of anxiety during unemployment is caused by money. With the possible exception of temporary unemployment compensation, we no longer have a steady income. Instead of money coming in, it is now slowly, sometimes not-so-slowly, draining away. Such shrinking finances make life seem very precarious, and it's very hard to be content with what seems to be disappearing.

But being content is exactly what the book of Hebrews tells us to do. And how are we to be content with what we have? By believing that Jesus will never leave us or forsake us—especially during unemployment. The source of our contentment is faith in the company of Christ.

We can do a few worldly things, however, to manage our level of anxiety over money. We can figure out creative ways to manage our finances the best we can. We can continue to keep up an active job search—filling out applications, following up on leads, going on interviews. We can take part-time work, if need be. If financial help is available from family, friends or community, we can ask for help. And when we've done our very best to take care of finances while seeking employment, we can simply look for contentment in the presence of Christ, who is always with us.

I am doing the best I can to manage my money
and look for work. Today I am content with what I have
because Jesus walks with me.

Doing What You Can

She has done what she could. . . .
—Mark 14:8

A dear friend of mine frequently used to quote this fragment from a verse from the Gospel according to Mark. She was mother to two busy children, a loving wife, career woman, and an active church leader. Although my friend was always going full speed just to keep up with the demands of her family, job, and church, she was constantly worried that somehow she wasn't doing enough. Jesus said of the woman bathing him with expensive perfume, "She has done what she could"—meaning that she was serving Jesus to the best of her ability by performing this one simple act. She didn't do the *most* she could; she did the *best* she could.

Unemployed people need to remember Jesus' praise of this woman. When worries and anxiety about being unemployed threaten to paralyze us, we can stop and ask ourselves four critical questions:

- Am I doing the very best I can to find another job?

- Am I managing my finances to the best of my ability?

- Am I getting the love and support I need from family and friends?

- Am I turning over to God circumstances and people I cannot directly control?

When the answers are "yes" to all of these questions, we can let go of worry and anxiety by repeating this short affirmation: "I'm doing the best I can; I have the love I need; I turn all the rest over to God."

When "no" is the answer to any of the above questions, we should stop wasting precious emotional energy on worry and instead use that energy to improve our efforts, ask for love, and turn over the uncontrollable to God.

At the end of today, may I hear Christ's voice
telling me I have done what I could.

Taking a Walk

. . . and Jesus was walking in the temple,
in the portico of Solomon.
—John 10:23

In the midst of the tempest that characterized so much of his ministry, Jesus takes time to savor the moment—he takes a walk through the portico of Solomon. I love the image of Jesus strolling through the temple; he takes time out from controversy and crisis to live fully in the present moment.

There is wisdom in living in the present for those of us who are unemployed. All we really have is the present—the past is finished, and while we are being responsible doing the best we can to find another job, the future is ultimately in God's hands alone. Living each day on its own terms is a far better use of our emotional and physical energy than uselessly trying to predict the future or rewrite the past.

Living in the present moment takes a little practice. Perhaps, like Jesus, walking helps keep me firmly anchored in the present moment. This sort of walking does not have a destination. It has no other purpose than to put one foot in front of the other, opening our senses to the sights, smells, and sounds of each moment.

You may wish to try this little walking exercise as a way of practicing the art of living one day at a time. Simply take a nice, slow walk. Consciously think about placing one foot deliberately in front of the other for the first ten minutes or so. Then become conscious of your breathing—take a few deep, easy breaths. Let your mind focus on what you smell, and on the colors and patterns you see. Before you know it, you are living each moment as it comes, leaving to God past hurts and future concerns.

Today is enough for me. Like Jesus, I'll take a
break from crisis and go for a walk.

The Path of Life

**You show me the path of life. In your presence there
is fullness of joy; in your right hand
are pleasures forevermore.
—Psalm 16:11**

Joy can be as near as God's presence. Unemployment threatens our present joy by diverting our attention to the past or causing us to obsess about the future. Too often unspoken questions like these circle around and around in our heads: "Will I ever work again?" "Where will I be in six months?" "Will the money hold out?" There are no real answers, and tomorrow seems so uncertain. An antidote to the anxiety unemployment brings is paying attention to the joy and pleasures of God's presence right now in the present moment.

I have a good friend who is frequently overwhelmed by the future and the complexity of her life. She used to say to me, "All I can do is live today in ten minute increments." And she did. She broke down each day into living ten minutes at a time. Doing so helped keep her anchored in the present. In those ten-minute increments she was able to find God's presence and enjoy it.

Joy and pleasure needn't wait until we have a job again. We don't need to borrow trouble from tomorrow when there is so much goodness right before us. The God who shows us the path of life is near, right now, today.

*You show me the path of life. In your presence there is fullness
of joy; in your hands are pleasures forevermore.*

Interior Glance

**The angel replied, "I am Gabriel. I stand in the presence
of God, and I have been sent to speak to you
and to bring you this good news."**
—Luke 1:19

Each day is angelic—each day is a messenger of God. Every day
we are unemployed, angels offer messages from the Holy One. Every
day brings good news—messages of inspiration, guidance, and most
of all, love. Whether we can hear those messages depends on our
willingness to listen carefully and patiently. We can't afford to miss
any messages of love, especially while we're living between jobs.
We need all the love and support we can get, not only from family
and friends, but from God as well. Each moment of every day is
holy and is not to be wasted regretting the past or worrying about
the future.

Listening to God's messages each moment takes a little practice.
Brother Lawrence, a seventeenth-century monk, knew the holiness
of each day. He knew every moment was overflowing with the good
news, the love of God. But Brother Lawrence also knew how easy it
is to forget God's love, which whispers to us every day. He practiced
what he called "the little interior glance"—the simple act of remembering, of noticing God's love for us in the moment.

We, too, can practice "the little interior glance" to understand
God's daily message of love. Each little interior glance is a simple
moment of opening up to the love of God. Many glances of God's
love come and go throughout the day. We can't afford to miss any
good news. Making little interior glances throughout the day opens
our hearts to a loving, guiding Lord.

*Today is angelic because each moment is filled to
overflowing with the love of God.*

Today Is Enough

"So do not worry about tomorrow,
for tomorrow will bring worries of its own.
Today's trouble is enough for today."
—Matthew 6:34

Not too long ago, a friend bluntly told me that my biggest enemy in life is dread of the future. She said, "You must fight dread with every ounce of your being or it will pull you down and you'll never surface under the weight of it." I suffer in particular from an irrational fear of tomorrow.

"I won't get that interview." "They'll never offer me enough money." "What if I don't get that job?" We've all heard ourselves talking or thinking along these lines. It all boils down to the fact that we're scared that we can't control tomorrow, and if we can't control it bad things will happen. Dread is literally a heavy feeling, and it weighs us down if we indulge in it for any length of time. Jesus has an antidote for those of us who've experienced any dread during unemployment. We must stop borrowing tomorrow's trouble in order to cope with today.

Today is enough. Coping with today keeps us from rocketing into tomorrow to find something bad and then bringing that trouble back into our lives today. *Today* is enough. Christ's words fill us with freedom and a sense of lightness because all we are responsible for is today. God can take care of tomorrow. Today *is enough.* Believing this keeps us from driving the people we love crazy with our outlandish, doom-filled predictions. We no longer have to predict anything. *Today is enough.* Jesus is Lord of the present and the future. Living for today is a miracle.

Today is enough. God will take care of tomorrow.

For the Good of All

**So then, whenever we have an opportunity,
let us work for the good of all, and especially for
those of the family of faith.
—Galatians 6:10**

We have the power to make many opportunities during our
unemployment. While looking for a job, we do everything we can to
create opportunities for ourselves by networking and following up
on leads from friends and professional acquaintances. We wouldn't
think of wasting any opportunity that may lead to employment.
Making and taking advantage of employment opportunities is part of
any responsible job search.

However, other kinds of opportunities are available during
unemployment. Each day there are opportunities to "work for
the good of all, and especially for those of the the family of faith." We
can take advantage of opportunities to minister to our churches and
communities, offering our skills and abilities for the well-being of
many. All too often we ignore the ministry opportunities each day
brings. Again and again I find myself postponing ministry until some
vague date in the future when I'm employed once again. Sometimes
I catch myself thinking, "I'll take some time for ministry once I'm in
a new job." Or I punish myself with the thought that if I were
really doing my best to find a job I'd be hired by now. So I feel
I must work harder, harder, harder!"

Just because we're unemployed doesn't mean we have to stop
living. We can create opportunities to help others each day. We have
power over our schedules, and we can schedule regular time to serve.

*Today I'll take advantage of an opportunity
to serve the good of all.*

Wait with Patience

**But if we hope for what we do not see,
we wait for it with patience.
—Roman 8:25**

Paul's letter to the Romans tells us that it is precisely because we can't see that we must have patience, for we hope for what we cannot see. Our hope is in nothing less than God's redemption of all creation, and we must wait for that redemption. In that hope we have patience. We need the same kind of patience during unemployment, when we can't see whatever may be just around the corner or still a long way off. Patience breeds hope, which overcomes despair.

We must also remember that God is always patient with us. I've found that it's helpful to try to be as patient with myself as God is. This means focusing on the positive—on the skills, abilities, and talents I have to offer not only potential employers, but also family, friends, church, and community. Being patient with myself means concentrating on what I'm doing well right now and rewarding myself for doing my best to find a new job, rather than beating myself up for still being unemployed. Being patient with myself means I take care of myself—asking for the emotional support I need from family and friends, eating well and getting some exercise, and making sure I regularly schedule social engagements. Finally, being patient with myself means knowing what I can control during unemployment and turning over to God that which I cannot control.

We must show ourselves infinite patience. Being patient with ourselves, as God is patient with us, will call out all that is best and good in us, and give us the energy we need to survive this difficult time.

*I have infinite patience with myself, for I hope
in what I cannot see.*

Practicing Patience

With patience a ruler may be persuaded,
and a soft tongue can break bones.
—Proverbs 25:15

It doesn't take any great insight to point out that being unemployed is incredibly difficult. It is natural and entirely appropriate to want unemployment to end as soon as possible. All too often, though, we fall into the subtle trap of thinking that the more we punish ourselves the faster we'll find a job and our unemployment will finally end. I sometimes find I've slipped into the mistaken belief that if I worry more and keep my anxiety level really high, I'll motivate myself to speed up the job search. Or I relentlessly pile on the pressure by telling myself I've got to hurry up and try harder and harder, so I won't have to be unemployed anymore.

"With patience a ruler may be persuaded, and a soft tongue can break bones." We can get more using a carrot than a stick. There is strength in gentleness. Punishing ourselves with useless worry or unrealistic expectations only makes being unemployed feel like an unrelieved agony. And it's no fun for those we live with either. Nobody wants to be around people who beat themselves up all the time. Self-punishment never solves anything, and it won't solve unemployment.

Patience, on the other hand, makes living between jobs much easier. When we are patient with ourselves, we refuse to waste precious emotional energy on worry or unrealistic expectations. Practicing patience is resting in the knowledge that we are doing the very best we can under trying circumstances. Being patient means gently giving ourselves a break. When we are busy practicing patience with ourselves we are able to enjoy life. And those we love are able to enjoy us.

Today I can look for work because I am patient with myself.

Holy Play

**Then shall the young women rejoice in the dance,
and the young men and the old shall be merry. I will turn
their mourning into joy, I will comfort them,
and give them gladness for sorrow.
—Jeremiah 31:13**

G. K. Chesterton once wrote that "joy is the serious business of heaven." Joy is holy play. Joy expressed in playfulness is a physical celebration of God's gift of life. We usually think that play is an activity for children only. But the art of play is important in adult life as well. Unemployment is a struggle for survival, and play helps us survive by focusing and celebrating that which is joyful in our lives. Unemployment brings plenty of stress and anxiety, but play helps relieve that stress and gives us a break from anxiety.

Play is any activity that helps us express the joy of being alive. It is whatever puts us in touch with life and helps us see that living each moment to the fullest is holier. It is more important than the fact that we don't have a job. For some, sports is a natural outlet for joy and play. For others, playing a musical instrument or gardening serve as a kind of play time. An unemployed friend of mine enjoys making pottery. He tells me that throwing pots is a creative act that is life-giving. When he steps up to his potter's wheel, the worry and stress of being unemployed subside and he feels as though he is participating in something much bigger than himself. As for me, I need people with whom to play and share my joy. Play can be a solitary activity or a social occasion—whatever helps us celebrate the life God gives us.

Play is not a luxury while we live between jobs—it is a necessity. It reaffirms the promise from Scripture, "I will turn their mourning into joy, I will comfort them, and give them gladness for sorrow."

My joy in being alive in God will be celebrated today in play.

Persevering in Prayer

**Rejoice in hope, be patient
in suffering, persevere in prayer.
—Romans 12:12**

Being unemployed sometimes gives me tunnel vision. I focus narrowly on looking for a job to the exclusion of all else in my life. During those times, I lose the big picture about who I am becoming, what I want, and how I can connect meaningfully with others and God. In other words, I lose sight of the fact that I am a human being on a journey toward Christ, regardless of my employment status.

Perseverance in prayer eliminates tunnel vision. As communication and union with God, prayer broadens our perspective, it returns to us the whole picture of our humanity. Our prayers do not ignore the fact that we are unemployed and need a job to survive. But after a period of time spent regularly in prayer, we begin to see that there are many different parts to our lives, including our working lives, that desire healing and wholeness.

As we persevere in prayer, we begin to bring much more than a request for a job before God. Many different parts of our lives, many other concerns and joys, are given voice in prayer. We speak with God about being parents, lovers, neighbors, friends, and disciples of Christ. We share with God the current state of our inner lives— happy, sad, worried, joyful, despairing, hopeful, or content. In prayer, we see that we are hosts to a great variety of relationships and emotions. In prayer we awaken a desire to be whole, for all of the complicated moving parts of our inner and outer lives to fit comfortably together. And in prayer we learn that, though finding a job is very important, it is still only one part of our lives in need of healing. We learn that through the work of prayer God is at work in all aspects of our lives, helping us to become whole in Christ.

*Today I persevere in prayer and offer all of myself to God,
asking that my desire for wholeness be honored.*

Heartfelt Meditations

**Let the words of my mouth and the meditation
of my heart be acceptable to you, O Lord,
my rock and my redeemer.
—Psalm 19:14**

Anybody who thinks being unemployed is time spent lying around and being lazy is crazy. Looking for work can be a full-time job. Making ends meet during unemployment takes a tremendous amount of creativity and drive. And when downtime does occur in our schedules, focusing on the positive and minimizing anxiety takes a lot of energy. In short, being unemployed is a very active, and busy time.

We need balance in our lives. Periods of intense activity and giving need to be balanced with periods of quietness and reflection about God. We need time in which we are receiving instead of giving. We need time for meditation. Meditation is the art of receiving—of accepting truth about ourselves, the world, and God. That is why the invocation, "Let the words of my mouth and the meditation of my heart be acceptable to you, O Lord" is so important; in meditation we are about to receive Christ. Meditation may involve using words from the Bible or even a novel or poem, prayer or union with God, or music that is special to us. Even the act of doing something we love, such as gardening or working out, may open us to receive Christ's grace.

Taking a moment to meditate on receiving the grace of Christ refreshes and restores our spirits. Small, quiet moments spent in meditation, receiving and accepting the truth of grace, balance all the giving and activity required of us.

*Let the words of my mouth and the meditation of my heart be
acceptable to you, O Lord, my rock and my redeemer.*

Being Quiet

But I have calmed and quieted my soul,
like a weaned child with its mother; my soul is like
the weaned child that is with me.
—Psalm 131:2

It is critical to surviving unemployment that we set aside regular times in our schedules to be quiet. I don't mean mere silence; outward silence is only the first step. Being quiet means experiencing inner quiet and peace, a calming of our souls. It means drowning out any thoughts inside our heads urging us to do something "significant" or become somebody important. It means taking a little rest in contemplation or prayer. The image in Psalm 131 of a child quietly resting on her mother's breast is tender and inviting. We are all God's children. Whether our schedules are crowded or not, we need to get a little peace and quiet with our heavenly parent—with God.

Being quiet with God doesn't have to take up a whole day. It can happen in the time it takes to arrange a bowl of flowers, write a note or say a prayer. And we don't have to become absolutely still and immobile, unless we want to. Quieting and calming our souls means we give those urgent pushing voices a rest while we do something reflective and restorative. Quiet time is nourishing if it lets us get in touch, even briefly, with who God has made us to be. A quiet soul gives us renewed energy and a renewed sense of ourselves. It secures us in God's love.

Being unemployed is such an urgent time. But we can calm and quiet our souls like a weaned child with its mother. Our souls can be the weaned child within us.

There is time to quietly rest in God today.

Letting Go in Prayer

**Hear my prayer, O Lord; give ear to my
supplications in your faithfulness; answer me
in your righteousness.
—Psalm 143:1**

Julian of Norwich wrote, "Pray inwardly, even if you do not enjoy it. It does good, though you feel nothing. Yes, even though you think you are doing nothing."

True prayer is letting go. True prayer places in the hands of God all of our needs and desires and leaves them there. For those of us who are unemployed, such prayer is an absolute necessity. It frees us of the compulsion to try controlling uncontrollable aspects of our situation. Prayer gives us instead the opportunity to be completely honest with God about what we want and need, and then let go.

This is why Julian of Norwich advised that we pray even when we *feel* nothing or think we are *doing* nothing. True communication with God always transforms us. Letting go in prayer frees us from being our own divinities, running our own little universes. True prayer changes us into human beings who trust in God's hope and power. We may feel nothing, for we think we are doing nothing when we pray. But in prayer we are quietly being restored to sanity.

"Pray inwardly, even if you do not enjoy it." Even if you do not enjoy giving up control. Even if you sometimes do not enjoy being entirely sane.

*Today I pray, let go, and let God quietly clothe
me in my right mind.*

Help!

**But she came and knelt before him,
saying, "Lord, help me."
—Matthew 15:25**

When I talk to my other unemployed friends, I sometimes express the deep desire to "stand on my own two feet" again. I want to work again so I can be self-sufficient. There is nothing wrong with wanting to stand on our own two feet, so long as we recognize that none of us really ever stands alone. The Caananite woman who begged for Jesus to heal her child recognized this fact. With courage and boldness she knelt and asked for help.

Family, friends, God, church, communities and government agencies are there to offer help and support when times are tough. Independence is no virtue when substituted for help, emotional or financial, that is really needed. That is not independence—it's just plain foolishness.

We do not love ourselves when we refuse to express our needs to God and loved ones. Asking for help is a sign of healthy self-esteem, not weakness. It means we value ourselves enough to want to continue surviving and growing. It also shows that we trust and value our relationship with God enough to be vulnerable.

There are certain to be times during unemployment when we each will need a little emotional or financial help. We won't compromise our self-sufficiency and independence by sharing our needs with God and others. Instead we'll see in a small way how all of us are connected to the Caananite woman and to each other.

*If I need help today, I will ask God and others
for it simply, proudly.*

Simple Hospitality

**Do not forsake your friend or the friend of your parent;
do not go to the house of your kindred in the day of your
calamity. Better is a neighbor who is nearby than
kindred who are far away.
—Proverbs 27:10**

Supportive relationships are our most important asset. The writer of Proverbs knew that. The quality of our relationships with friends and family determines the quality of our lives during calamities. Maintaining caring, loving relationships is how we experience the emotional support and stability we need. Cultivating new friendships and acquaintances develops a network that may offer leads on possible employment, as well as new relationships based on genuine caring and understanding.

A Jewish proverb says, "Hospitality is one form of worship." Hospitality is a way of expressing gratitude to God for the blessings of love and friendship. It is a way of affirming the goodness of life, even when times are tough. Practicing hospitality keeps us connected to other people that God sends our way, others who make our lives rich with their presence.

For me, offering hospitality to friends and loved ones has been a lifeline during unemployment. Making my home a comfortable, cheerful place where I welcome friends is how I cultivate and maintain loving relationships. Because I live on a fairly tight budget, the hospitality I offer is simple, yet it is appreciated. Hospitality need not be elaborate, only heart-felt, welcoming, and fun. And when I offer hospitality to others, I too feel supported and loved. I may be unemployed, but the quality of my life, which includes relationships that make life worth living, is very rich.

*Unemployment does not diminish the quality of my life. I offer
simple hospitality to friends, who make my life rich.*

Wisdom and Knowledge

God answered Solomon, "Because this was in
your heart, and you have not asked for possessions,
wealth, honor, or the life of those who hate you, and have
not even asked for long life, but have asked for wisdom and
knowledge for yourself that you may rule my people
over whom I have made you king, wisdom and
knowledge are granted to you."
—2 Chronicles 1:11-12

Free of defining ourselves by what we do for a living, we now have the opportunity to find out who *we* really are on the inside. Solomon's request of God for wisdom and knowledge is not necessarily what we might expect from a career politician. In shunning the kingly trappings of wealth, revenge, and honor, Solomon revealed the kind of man he really was on the inside. And God rewarded him.

We can ask ourselves these same kinds of exploratory questions:

- What do I believe about myself now that I am unemployed?
- What am I most afraid of?
- What am I most excited and happy about?
- How do I feel about my family and friends?
- What kind of person do I want to become?
- Who can I turn to for support and caring?
- What is God calling me to do with my life?
- What have I learned in my relationship with God?

Looking for the answers is an exciting journey in self-discovery and spiritual growth. It's easy to ask God for wealth, possessions, and honor. It's harder to ask God for the riches of knowledge and wisdom. But in the long run, it's much more rewarding.

God grant me wisdom and knowledge today.

One Thing Needful

**The Lord answered her, "Martha, Martha, you are worried
and distracted by many things; there is need of only one
thing. Mary has chosen the better part, which will
not be taken away from her."
—Luke 10:41-42**

Here is the story of two women I know, each in their early for-
ties. Both took advantage of their situation to take a good, hard look
at their lives. Each woman wrestled with one of the hardest questions
to answer, "What do I really want to do with my life?" And each
discovered she wanted to write more than anything else in the world.

One of the women, a single mother with a mortgage to pay,
decided to risk everything and act on her newly acquired self-
knowledge. She worked hard, built up a professional network, and
became a full-time free-lance writer and editor. She is now quite
content with her life because she is doing the one thing she really
wants to do.

The other woman, also single, had no debts to speak of. But
instead of fashioning a career on her love of writing, she settled for
a full-time job she didn't like in the marketing department of a
large corporation. She knew what she wanted to do with her life
but decided to play it safe and not risk the financial insecurity of
building a writing career. Today this woman still dislikes her marketing job, yet continues to ignore pursuing the job that would bring
her happiness.

Each of us must examine ourselves and decide what is necessary
for us to be happy in a future occupation.

*Lord, guide me and give me strength
to do the one thing needful.*

Secret Space

**But whenever you pray, go into your room
and shut the door and pray to your Father who is
in secret; and your Father who sees in
secret will reward you.
—Matthew 6:6**

When we were employed, many of us had our own physical space in which to do our job—an office, a cubicle, a work station, a desk. That work space was a place where we made decisions or produced something. It was a space where we were in control.

Now that the work space is gone, it is essential that we create a new work space for ourselves during unemployment. Having such a space helps us continue to feel like professionals. This space becomes the control center for maintaining an active job search, doing temporary or free-lance work, or just dreaming. It's like the room Jesus spoke of—a space to bear our souls to God our creator, a space to dream with God about who we are to become.

My own work space consists of 4 x 5 feet in my bedroom, with a small table, a small computer and printer, and a few office supplies. No one else is allowed within this 4 x 5 area—it is mine alone. This work space gives form to my dreams. In this little space I dream with God about what I want to do with the next part of my life and I pursue appropriate employment leads.

We all need to go into our room, a place where we can connect with God and direct our lives. Create a space that helps you dream about the next chapter in your life and helps you pursue that dream.

*Today I dream with God about what
to do with my working life.*

Strength from God

**O my strength, I will watch for you; for you,
O God, are my fortress.
—Psalm 59:9**

Where does the strength to weather a crisis like unemployment come from? Strength has two sources. The first comes from God, who strengthens our hearts, minds, and bodies to cope with whatever comes. God's gift to us is that refusal to give up because we know that somehow "this, too, shall pass." Crises, by their very definition, are temporary, and with God's strength and perseverance we will be employed again.

The second source of strength also comes from God. God gives us strength through one or more persons who believe in us. These people refuse to believe that we will succumb to the present crisis or that we will not be able to overcome various obstacles to employment. These people are channels of God's strength to us because they believe in our talents, skills, and potential. In other words, they look at us, see the best, and tell us so.

We need access to both sources of God's strength during unemployment. We must blend an inner attitude of "never say die" with God's promise of strength. Our inner strength and resolve is kept strong when we spend time with people who affirm God's gifts in us. We simply cannot survive unemployment alone. Strength to weather unemployment comes from simple perseverance and seeking out the company of those who believe in us.

*Today I will seek both sources of the strength
that comes from God.*

Inner Life

**Hear, O Israel: the Lord our God, is one; you shall love
the Lord your God with all your heart, and with
all your soul, and with all your mind, and
with all your strength.
—Mark 12:29-30**

Evelyn Underhill wrote that "after all it is those who have a deep
and real inner life who are best able to deal with the 'irritating details
of outer life.'" Cultivating "a deep and real inner life" helps each
of us to cope with the frustration and anxiety of unemployment.
The wellspring of that inner life is the greatest commandment,
"Hear, O Israel: the Lord our God, is one; you shall love the Lord
your God with all your heart, and with all your soul, and with all
your mind, and with all your strength." An inner life fueled by the
love of God supplies us with the strength we need to live each day.

An all-consuming love of God gives us a kind of strength beyond
our ability to cope while we are living between jobs. In a strange,
mystical way our inner life gives us a new, valuable perspective on
unemployment. We realize there's a great big universe out there
and we each have a life to live in it for our God, ourselves, and one
another. When we allow ourselves to tap into the greatest, most
primal of all God's commandments, we are better able to cope with
the frustration and anxiety unemployment brings. And we find that
we have the strength to cope with another day.

*The Lord our God is one; and today I love the Lord our God
with all my heart, soul, mind, and strength.*

The Gift of Survival

**Then the remnant of Jacob, surrounded by many peoples,
shall be like dew from the Lord, like showers on
the grass, which do not depend upon people
or wait for any mortal.**
—Micah 5:7

The word *remnant* is the biblical word for survivors. Micah prophesied that Israel would be led away into captivity in Babylon. But there was comfort in Micah's prophesy—a remnant would survive captivity and one day return to their own land.

God is interested in the survival of his people. One way God provides for our survival is through our work. We work to provide for our families and keep a roof over our heads. Whether we are considering a career transition or are unemployed, simply continuing to survive is a sign of courage and faith in the love of God who does not depend upon people or wait for any mortal.

There are many sources of joy that enable us to survive while we search for new work. If we listen to our hearts, we hear the voice of God offering care and support to his remnant, and we recognize what our resources are.

Make a list today of the people, activities, and resources available to you that help you to survive. Put the list where you can consult it regularly. Remember that God is passionately concerned about your survival, and you *will* survive.

*I am one of God's chosen people, his remnant.
Today God gives me the gift of survival.*

Irrevocable Gifts

. . . the gifts and the calling of God are irrevocable.
—Romans 11:29

Being unemployed sometimes makes us question our God-given gifts. After my first few rejections by potential employers I began to doubt my experience, skills, and talents. I also learned that I could not dwell in self-doubt for very long. I had to project absolute confidence in my abilities at the next interview.

I found that the best antidote to self-doubt was to trust that "the gifts and the calling of God are irrevocable." Friends and my job-search support group have helped immensely in developing that trust. These people continually affirm my skills and God's love for me. They help me see that I have talents that are attractive to potential employers. Such external affirmation helps me to trust the God who calls and cares for me.

God has given each one of us gifts. Listening to the affirmation and encouragement of friends helps us believe in our unique blessings. When we trust God, listen to those who love us, and take a fresh look at our own life experiences, new gifts reveal themselves, and new doors open.

I trust that God's gifts to me are irrevocable.

Self-Discipline

**Therefore prepare your minds for action; discipline
yourselves; set all your hope on the grace that Jesus Christ
will bring you when he is revealed.
—1 Peter 1:13**

Our jobs used to provide us with discipline. We arrived at work
at a certain time and performed various tasks throughout the day
before returning home. Now that we are unemployed we must
provide discipline for ourselves to keep our minds active and build
hope in the grace of Christ.

Discipline is using our time wisely to channel our best energies
toward accomplishing our goals—and building hope. Without discipline, our best energy is drained away because it has no focus. I know
a recently unemployed man who uses no discipline to regulate how
he spends his time. He might, for instance, spend a lot of energy
worrying about not finding a job because he spent most of his week
procrastinating. Or he gets exhausted and discouraged because he
packed one week to the brim with interviews and job searches, but
neglected to schedule any business appointments or interviews for
the following week.

Balance is the hallmark of good discipline. Disciplined time spent
looking for a job, preparing résumés, making phone calls, and
interviewing should be balanced with time for self-reflection, prayer,
meditation, exercise, fun, and relaxation, so our energies are spread
as evenly as possible. Simply making a balanced schedule brings activity and discipline to our days. We won't eliminate anxiety from our
lives, but building discipline will prevent us from careening on an
emotional roller coaster, divorced from hope in Christ.

*I am disciplined today. My energy is focused toward accomplishing
today's goals and building my hope in the grace of Christ.*

Today Is the Day

. . . See, now is the acceptable time; see,
now is the day of salvation!
—2 Corinthians 6:2

Sometimes boredom is unavoidable when we are between jobs. The old daily routine and tasks that occupied our working schedules no longer fill our days. Even though we maintain an active job search, we still occasionally experience periods of down time, times when there just isn't much happening on the job front. Then boredom can set in and time becomes the enemy.

But time is not really our enemy. Each day is a gift meant to be lived to its fullest—"now is the acceptable time; see, now is the day of salvation!" During down times, we need to have a strategy that changes a meaningless day into a day of salvation.

I have a friend who is prepared for those down times. When her job search is at a stage where there isn't much activity, she battles boredom and frustration by attending self-improvement seminars. She enrolls in seminars that either help her with her job search or help her explore who she is and what she wants to do with her life. My friend also maintains an active reading schedule, and she keeps up a very active social life.

Time is not the enemy, but boredom and frustration are. Having a plan like my friend's makes each day a holy day to be lived fully. Now is the time to keep our spirits up and channel energy into positive, life-enhancing endeavors.

Today is the day of salvation.
I will not waste today with boredom.

Holy Time

**The time is fulfilled, and the kingdom of God
has come near; repent, and believe in the good news.
—Mark 1:15**

Life is precious and time is not meant to be wasted. We'll find that it is impossible to waste time when we perceive and experience the holiness in each day. We may spend the day actively in interviewing for jobs and sending out résumés, or we may spend it passively by sitting quietly in a park. Neither day is a waste of time when we glimpse the kingdom of God. John the Baptist's words are for us—"The time is fulfilled, and the kingdom of God has come near."

Benedictine monks glimpse the holiness of every day. This is not because they are religious professionals, but because they believe that whether they are busy at work or out taking a walk in the countryside, God sees every life-enhancing activity as holy work for God's kingdom.

Such a daily experience of the holy is available to all of us, not just monks. It's not the quantity of tasks and activities that reveal the holiness in each day, it's the quality of those activities that open us up to the goodness of God. It is impossible to waste time when we begin each day believing that God sees each life-enhancing act as holy. If looking for a job today enhances our lives, then whatever we do today to find a job is tinged with holiness. If visiting a new exhibit at the museum enhances our lives today, we prepare ourselves to view the holy. If having coffee with a friend enhances life today, look for holiness reflected in your friend's eyes.

Look for the holy in every moment of every day. When we begin each day expecting to glimpse the holy by looking at the quality of the activities that fill our day, precious time is never wasted. And each moment becomes a small act of worship.

Today is holy. Let me glimpse the holy in everything I do.

Surpassing Value

. . . I regard everything as loss because of the surpassing
value of knowing Christ Jesus my Lord. For his sake I have
suffered the loss of all things, and I regard them as
rubbish, in order that I may gain Christ.
—Philippians 3:8

The next time you are at a party where you are meeting new people, try to refrain from asking what they do for a living. It is practically impossible because our society has trained us to define ourselves and others by the work we do. Often we value each other based on what kind of contribution we make to the community, on how useful we are to our society, on how much power we have in our jobs, or on how much money we are accumulating. If our work is considered by society to be somewhat ordinary, or if we are unemployed, we are often tempted to undervalue ourselves.

While work is important, it does not really define who we are as human beings. For Christians, everything is regarded as loss when compared to "the surpassing value of knowing Christ Jesus." We are much more than what we do for a living. By the grace of Christ we are holy children of the living God. This is first and primarily who we really are. As holy people, we are called to love well, build healthy relationships, rejoice in the variety of God's creation, and explore the wonders of our own grace-filled souls.

Letting go of a compulsive need to define our value only in terms of our jobs is like letting go of rubbish. It's well-ridden in comparison to the surprising value of knowing Christ Jesus, our Lord. Only when we experience Christ's love for us can we realize our value as human beings infinitely loved by our Creator.

Today I regard everything as loss because of the surpassing
value of knowing Christ Jesus my Lord.

Being Transformed

**And all of us, with unveiled faces, seeing the glory of the
Lord as though reflected in a mirror, are being transformed
into the same image from one degree of glory to another;
for this comes from the Lord, the Spirit.
—2 Corinthians 3:18**

Unemployment is a time of transformation. When we are living
between jobs, we are in the process of transforming or changing
one source of employment into another. But transformation is
much more than simply switching jobs. Transformation requires a
reorientation of our souls toward love, a removing of our veiled
views of life to come face to face with the Spirit's glory.

Unemployment offers us the time needed for transformation. In
the absence of our former work and our old ways of defining ourselves by what we did for a living, we can reexamine our values. Now
we now have the luxury of truly asking and answering, "What and
who do I love most in my life?" and "How do I act on that love?"
Now we have the time to plan and follow action that can turn our
lives around 180 degrees and change us from one degree of glory
to another.

Identifying who and what we love, and acting on that knowledge, opens our very souls to transformation. We may have acted as
Christians before. God opens our very souls to transformation. Our
unemployment may be offering us now a once-in-a lifetime opportunity to refocus and reorient our souls toward living love to a degree
we never imagined possible. If we pursue this love and gain even a
mere reflection of God's glory, we may forever consider our time of
unemployment the greatest blessing we ever experienced. And we
may begin to understand what God, who *is* love, is all about and why
acting on God's love is the most important thing we can do.

*Today I begin reorienting my soul toward love by identifying
who and what I love, and acting on that knowledge.*

Open to the New

**For I am about to create new heavens
and a new earth; and the former thing shall not
be remembered or come to mind.
—Isaiah 65:17**

I have a friend who frequently wears a T-shirt which proclaims, "He who hesitates is lunch. See Charles Darwin." In a time of ever-changing, often uncertain economic conditions, the saying "what worked once must always work" is a prescription for extinction. For several months after I lost my job, I refused to part with what I perceived to be my brightest hour. While working in my old job, I firmly believed I had arrived. I *knew* I would remain in my chosen career for the rest of my working life. But the economy and the company for which I worked changed drastically. I lost my job. And since then, the industry in which I seek to continue my career staggers and reels from permanently shifting economic realities. Does any of this sound familiar?

God is also always creating something completely new. Our God is not a god of the status quo. Creation brings change. Spiritually we must remain flexible and willing to adapt to whatever new thing God is creating in our lives, especially with regard to our employment. Many of us are considering careers we had never dreamed of before. Perhaps our brightest hours are not in the past but are still yet to come. Who knows what wonderful surprises God has in store for us? God is creating "new heavens and a new earth." We don't want to miss it! The future may hold new blessings for us.

*My survival depends on being flexible and adaptable. Today I let
go of any "bright hours" that keep me rigidly tied to the past
so that I can see the new handiwork of God.*

Confidence in Christ

**Therefore do not throw away your confidence,
which has a great reward. For you have need of endurance,
so that you may do the will of God and
receive what was promised.
—Hebrews 10:35-36**

Confidence is the key to surviving and thriving during unemployment. With a strong sense of confidence in Jesus Christ we can overcome virtually anything. We can cultivate that confidence when we remember to tell ourselves three things:

First, God cares and provides for us. God is working good in our lives right now. Signs of God's care are all around us in the faces of those who love us and in our own spiritual growth and development. God provides for us right now in so many ways. Knowing that God through Jesus Christ is at work for good in our lives gives us hope and confidence.

Second, our unemployment is only temporary. Good things and bad things happen to us throughout our lives. Such seasons of good times and bad do not last forever. Only God is forever. Our mortal lives are filled with constant change. Unemployment, too, shall pass. Reminding ourselves that unemployment is seasonal rather than final renews our confidence in Christ.

Finally, there is much more to us than any skills or talents we may possess. Our confidence in Christ is rooted in the knowledge that we are valuable to God independent of any abilities or qualifications we may have. We are much more than any job. We are children of God, loved and cared for by Jesus Christ.

Today I am confident in Christ the Lord, who by his death and resurrection has shown me how valuable I am to God.

In God's Camp

**Jacob went on his way and the angels of God met
him; and when Jacob saw them he said,
"This is God's camp!"
—Genesis 32:1-2**

When I was in seminary, a friend always used to speak about the
importance of "inner resources" in dealing with the various challenges and obstacles that training for the ministry presented. At first
I had no idea what she meant. To me, resources were always external
things that helped me survive, such as food, housing, or a job. Later,
after surviving the various challenges and obstacles of seminary life,
I recognized inner resources I never knew I had.

Today I like to imagine that those inner resources are a host of
interior angels I meet as I go my way and that they empower me
to cope with unemployment. Whether or not these angels actually
exist, it is certain that God gives us inner strength, courage, hope,
humor, love, creativity, wisdom, gentleness, and perseverance to help
us overcome the challenges and obstacles unemployment presents us
every day. We call on these angels whenever we are afraid, anxious,
uncertain or feel like our lives are out of control.

An employed friend of mine is currently facing a profound crisis,
which not only threatens his career but also threatens his health. This
mellow, even-tempered friend recently told me that his stress level
has shot off the chart. And I heard fear and deep pain in his voice.
With no viable options open to him, my friend calls on God daily for
courage and fortitude to help him "gut out" the crisis.

Like my friend, we can call on God's protection and inner
resources. They will bear us up on wings of promise to meet each day
with pride and dignity.

*I am in God's camp, and he will send me whatever resources
I need to cope with unemployment today.*

The Narrow Door

**Strive to enter through the narrow door;
for many, I tell you, will try to enter
and will not be able.
—Luke 13:24**

Jesus invites us to enter the narrow door that leads to a deeper experience of faith. The narrow door may be small and skinny—but it is not locked. Rather, it is an open door to anyone with the courage to step through.

Unemployment is a kind of narrow, open door. Such a door is a traditional symbol of opportunity—an invitation to a better life. But viewing unemployment as an inviting, open door involves more than planning how to get a better job. To walk through unemployment's open door, we must have the courage to reexamine all that life has to offer and, if necessary, redefine ourselves and our relationships.

Now is the time to find out what we really want out of life, reassess our skills and talents, determine what we want from our relationships with family and friends, and plan how we can better nurture those relationships. Now is the time to ask God to guide our spiritual growth as human beings.

Unemployment is an open door, a chance for a new life. All the old rules, obligations and schedules that defined the days when we were employed no longer apply. Now we are free to luxuriate in the fresh air this open door lets into our lives. The door before us is narrow, but it stands open, issuing an invitation to a new way of living, loving, and working in the world.

*If I choose, I can walk through an open door and playfully
consider reshaping my life, faith, and loves.*

Opening Doors

**For everyone who asks receives, and everyone
who searches finds, and for everyone who knocks,
the door will be opened.
—Luke 11:10**

My mother once gave me an embroidery of the following senti-
ment: "When God closes one door, he opens another." However,
when one door closes on our happiness, we're usually so focused on
the door just slammed in our face that we find it hard to ask God
for another door to open, or we can't see the other doors God is
opening around us.

There may be plenty of open doors to new happiness all around
us even though we are presently staring at unemployment's locked
door. Those open doors may not include a new job just now, but
each invites us to enter and find happiness nonetheless. New, open
doors may offer a renewed appreciation and love of our families,
time to develop the creative side of ourselves, dreams of starting
a new business or changing careers, or the opportunity to go back
to school.

Each day God opens new doors. We have only to tear our eyes
away from the closed door in front of us and look around to explore
the happiness available to us while we are unemployed. There is no
question that having a job and the financial means to support ourselves and our families is incredibly important. Still, life is more than
simply having a job. We are much more than workers. Those open
doors invite us to explore the world around us, our relationships, and
our inner worlds to uncover whatever happiness awaits. One day, a
door will open to new employment. But until then, there are many
other doors to step through and find joy.

Today I ask God to open new doors for me.

Something Good

**If you then, who are evil, know how to give good
gifts to your children, how much more will your Father
in heaven give good things to those who ask him!
—Matthew 7:11**

Jesus tells us that the Father wants to give us "good things"—
we've only to ask him. Sometimes it's too easy to give ourselves guilt-
laden messages like "You've got to work a lot harder at finding a job"
or "That free time should be spent polishing up your résumé" or
"You shouldn't pamper yourself until you're working again."

I am determined to enjoy myself in spite of my unemployment.
Every couple of weeks, my unemployment support group gets
together to share a pot-luck, an occasion marked by laughter and
general silliness. I use e-mail on my computer to write a friend in
southern California—each of us tries to outdo the other at writing
amusing letters. I go to bargain matinees with another unemployed
friend. Since unemployment offers enough drama, we avoid seeing
serious movies in favor of watching comedies.

Too much of a good thing can be wonderful. We've only to ask
God for the gift of good things. Getting too much of a good thing is
just as important as getting a job—it restores us, refreshes us, and
reenergizes us for doing what needs to be done.

Father, today I ask for something good.

Choosing Happiness

**Then he looked up at his disciples and said:
"Blessed are you who are poor, for yours
is the kingdom of God."
—Luke 6:20**

The above verse comes from Luke's version of Jesus' Sermon on the Mount. The deeper meaning of the word "blessed" is "happy"—in other words, to be blessed by God is to be happy. Jesus turns happiness on its head—the hungry, the weeping, the poor, and the excluded are in reality happy because God has blessed them. In today's culture, we confuse happiness with circumstance—if our circumstances are good, if we have a job, plenty of money, food, and love, then happiness naturally results. Jesus says that true happiness lies in God's blessing regardless of circumstance.

Although we may be unemployed, we can be happy by making the decision to focus on what we already have in life by the grace of God as opposed to focusing on what's missing. It is choosing to see God's abundance in our lives instead of absence. It is to want what we have rather than be consumed by longing for what is not yet available. To live this way is to live a blessed life.

For me, worries about money always seem to prevent me from experiencing happiness. So I created a little ritual for myself each time I pay the bills. Every time I have the money to write a check, I consciously tell myself what a victory it is to meet this particular obligation. And I breathe a brief prayer of thanksgiving to God. I deliberately choose not to focus on the fact that I have virtually no disposable income or that the next bill may require some very creative juggling of funds. Instead, my little ritual helps me focus on the abundance out of which I am able to meet my financial obligations one at a time.

When we look for God's blessed abundance in the small, everyday details present in our lives, it becomes increasingly difficult to be unhappy over whatever may be missing. It is possible to live a happy, blessed life during unemployment.

*I choose to be happy today by identifying one area in my life
in which God has abundantly blessed me.*

Cheerful Hearts

**A glad heart makes a cheerful countenance, but by
sorrow of heart the spirit is broken.
—Proverbs 15:13**

Each of us has had anxious days when we just couldn't be happy
no matter how hard we tried. Well, if we can't be happy, we can still
be cheerful. Not the kind of fake cheerfulness that comes from deny-
ing the fact that we're unemployed and worried about money and
the future. No, cheerfulness born of denial isn't cheerfulness—it's
simple stupidity. The kind of cheerfulness of which this proverb
speaks is a kind of spiritual self-defense. We're unemployed. We have
problems. But we will not let our spirits be broken. We safeguard our
spirits with cheer.

Being cheerful doesn't make our problems disappear. It simply
makes life a little more pleasant for ourselves and those around us as
we continue to deal with those problems and concerns. Letting our
problems define our attitudes and feelings can really ruin an otherwise
good day. A decision to act cheerfully is a decision that refuses to let
our cares and worries get us down, and it rescues the day from total
disaster. It mysteriously supplies us with more energy to face up to our
problems and find creative, constructive solutions.

One of my best friends is a cheerful person. He has an extremely
stressful job and a very turbulent personal life. Each day he makes a
conscious decision to be cheerful. Over the years, I have watched
people develop an extraordinary loyalty to him—they naturally want
to be around someone so cheerful and down-right funny.

If we can't always be happy, we can defend our spirits and strive
always to be cheerful to make life a bit more pleasant for ourselves
and others, and to find the energy and emotional support we need to
cope successfully with unemployment.

*I choose a cheerful countenance today.
I will not deny my problems, but I choose to make life
more pleasant for me and those I love.*

Hope in God

May the God of hope fill you with all joy and peace in believing, so that you may abound in hope by the power of the Holy Spirit.
—Romans 15:13

Hope is the reason we get up every day when we're living between jobs. Hope is believing that God's goodness awaits us. It is believing that the Holy Spirit is working for good in our lives. Having hope is a tremendous source of power, energy and motivation. When we greet each day with a sense of hopefulness, we are ready for whatever good the new day may bring to our lives.

It is possible to encourage or cultivate hope. Encouraging hope means drawing on strength, even during those times when it seems we are weak and powerless. We feel strong when we focus on the gifts God gives us: talents and skills; intelligence and character; power and the ability to accomplish our goals; faith in God; the capacity for love and caring. We feel strong when we identify blessings present in our lives—our loved ones, homes, friendships, and the moments of beauty in the world around us.

Feeling strong also means taking care of our physical needs and regarding our bodies as temples of hope. I heartily dislike exercise. But after a bad day of feeling helpless or weak, I find taking a prolonged, very brisk walk simply makes me feel stronger. When I give my body much needed exercise, I experience my body as a tremendous gift from God. In other words, my strength begins to return and I can hope again.

We will occasionally feel powerless during unemployment. But even then we can feel strong again and hope again. Identifying and experiencing goodness already present in our lives contributes to feelings of strength and fills us with joy and peace in believing.

I am strong because I hope in God and am
empowered by the Holy Spirit.

Active Hope

**O Israel, hope in the Lord! For with the Lord
there is steadfast love, and with him
is great power to redeem.
—Psalm 130:7**

I used to think of hopefulness as a very passive virtue. But it isn't. Hope is intensely active. Hope, to believe that God can redeem difficult times, takes a lot of work. Hope is an activity, it is something we *do*. First, hope is actively gaining a new perspective about being unemployed. That means taking God's perspective, finding goodness already present in our lives, looking beyond our immediate circumstances to a loving God working for good in our lives, and gently anticipating that God's goodness can come from this period of unemployment.

Hope requires more than developing a new perspective—it simply isn't possible to maintain an attitude of hopefulness while we beat ourselves up over our failure to find employment. If we stop berating ourselves and instead treat ourselves to a little respect and gentleness, hope in God will return.

*Hope is active in my life today. I look beyond the surface of my life
for God's goodness. And, like God, I treat myself with
respect, patience, and gentleness.*

Boldly Hope

**Since, then, we have such a hope,
we act with great boldness. . . .
—2 Corinthians 3:12**

Hope must be pursued if it is to remain alive in our hearts. In hope we must "boldly go where no one has gone before." Pursuing hope is actively working to bring into existence whatever it is we hope for and realizing that ultimately our hope is in God.

The bold pursuit of hope is what sustains us during unemployment. When we pursue a new job, we pursue hope. Wedding our hope to action helps us feel more powerful. It helps keep fear at bay because there is something constructive we are doing to cope with, or even change, our circumstances.

We all have hopes besides securing employment. And these hopes, too, need pursuit. I continue boldly to pursue my hope of home ownership. I read the real estate section of the newspaper, follow fluctuations in interest rates, occasionally walk through open homes, and drive around neighborhoods in which I'd like to live— all in preparation for the day when I am able to afford a home. Because I boldly hope in God, I can boldly hope for a home.

When we honor our hopes by pursuing them, our hope in God is strengthened. And this strengthened hope gives us the boldness, power, and motivation to continue pursuing our hope.

*I am in bold pursuit of God's hope today. I draw power and
strength from God to make my hope a reality.*

New Identity

**Look at what is before your eyes. If you are confident that
you belong to Christ, remind yourself of this, that just
as you belong to Christ, so also do we.**
—2 Corinthians 10:7

It's tough belonging only to Christ. We have been accustomed
to "belonging" to what we do for a living. Now part of our identity
is gone. But only one part. Unemployment offers us a unique opportunity to get reacquainted with ourselves and our God without the
crutch of a job title. And we have schedules that are flexible enough
now to actually devote time to figuring out who we are in Christ.

Initially, my identity felt threatened when I no longer had a job.
I'd meet new people and feel awkward telling them I was unemployed in response to the perennial question, "What do you do for a
living?" But after a while, I began to discover that my identity rested
in Christ alone. I felt much more comfortable without the stress of
my old high-pressure job and enjoyed just being me in Christ.
Eventually, I was able to let go of needing to define myself by my job.

Now I enjoy what is good and valuable about simply being the
person God created me to be. It's a great feeling. Getting reacquainted with ourselves in Christ ultimately raises our self-esteem
and improves our outlook on our lives and relationships.

Today I belong to Christ alone; my identity lives in Jesus.

Called to Love

Love the Lord, all you his saints.
—Psalm 31:23

As God's chosen people, we are his saints. And as God's saints, we are called to love. This is not difficult because we know God first loved us, and we have many, many opportunities to love. Some are seemingly insignificant, yet they can mean so much.

A friend told me not long ago that while he was experiencing an extremely difficult time in his life, he shared his troubles over the phone with another friend who was unemployed and who lived on the other side of the country. Not long after they talked, witty cards and letters of encouragement began arriving from her weekly. The letters and cards were little ways in which she expressed her love and concern, but they touched my friend enormously and made him feel cared for in a special way.

This woman is one of God's saints, who loves the Lord by showing love to those in need. She is an example for all of us to follow. Even though we are unemployed, we can also express small kindnesses to friends in need of encouragement. We know what it's like to have a tough time and how we'd like to be treated while living between jobs.

I am God's saint, and today I show my love for the Lord
by doing little things for others.

Come and See

Nathanael said to him, "Can anything good come out of Nazareth?" Philip said to him, "Come and see."
—John 1:46

Perception is the ability to see with understanding. We see ourselves, others, and situations not only with our minds but also with our hearts. A cynical Nathanael rhetorically inquires whether anything good can come out of the insignificant town of Nazareth. And Philip answers, "Come and see."

Unemployment offers us the opportunity to deepen our perception of the miraculous. When we were employed, we worked on one side of a tapestry—the working world of routine, steady income, stress, accomplishment. Now we are working the other side of the same tapestry—searching for a job, juggling finances, fighting anxiety, exploring what we really want to do, making new relationships, strengthening old ones, opening ourselves to new possibilities, and taking nothing for granted. We perceive the world of work from both sides now. We also perceive God miraculously at work providing for us and loving us.

One of the most powerful lessons I've learned while unemployed is to never, ever take for granted God's gifts: our talents and abilities, church and home; family and friends. I have also learned to perceive these things with my heart. This newfound perception has also added compassion to my way of seeing the world, and I hold a special place in my heart for others who are without work. I no longer see them as unemployed people: now I also see a miracle, courage, resourcefulness, and perseverance. Unemployment has expanded, deepened, and matured my perception of God at work in the world.

Today I will come and see—see life with the eyes
of my heart, as well as the eyes of my head.
Today I will see miracles.

Beyond Control

**For Jews demand signs and Greeks desire wisdom,
but we proclaim Christ crucified, a stumbling block to Jews
and foolishness to Gentiles, but to those who are the
called, both Jews and Greeks, Christ the power
of God and the wisdom of God.
—1 Corinthians 1:22-24**

Unemployment is a time of great uncertainty. We are doing our best to find another job while making ends meet in the meantime. Still, being unemployed is a situation that sometimes feels beyond our control. For example, we may have an excellent interview with a potential employer. But we can't make anyone hire us. That decision is simply beyond our control. And because we are ultimately not in control of the situation, our anxiety level just shoots through the roof.

When life during unemployment begins to feel out of control, it's a comfort to know there is a God in whose care we can trust. Christ is the power of God over those uncontrollable forces in our lives. We experience this power when we stop trying to control the uncontrollable and trust in Christ's care and guidance. Giving up the need to control takes a little practice in trusting the wisdom of God as well. When I begin to obsess about the uncontrollable aspects of being unemployed, I have to turn those aspects over to God, having faith that Christ crucified is God's wisdom. Eventually, I am able to trust God enough to lessen my anxiety and get on with the parts of my life over which I have been given some control.

Unemployment is a time when we sometimes feel as though we are trying to find our way through a pathless world. But when the uncertainty and anxiety become too much, we can trust that the power and wisdom of God travels with us, guiding our way— wandering maybe, but not lost.

*There is much to being unemployed that is beyond my control.
I trust in the power and wisdom of God to lead me
through that which is uncontrollable.*

Strength to Care

God is our refuge and strength,
a very present help in trouble.
—Psalm 46:1

Acknowledging the power of God does not necessarily eliminate the fear and anxiety of being unemployed. Our relationship with God is not based on a wish or a bargain that will make life instantly okay again. Instead, it is complete trust that God will be our safe refuge and give us the strength to cope with the reality of unemployment—that God will be present and help us through these troubled times.

God does not promise to make everything better overnight. Rather, God promises to love us, provide for us, and to guide us no matter what happens in our lives. God promises to be our strength and to empower us to cope with the seemingly overwhelming challenges of being unemployed.

I am sometimes tempted to ask God to make me an emotional zombie. I want God to take away all the "bad" feelings of fear, anxiety, or sadness, and make me happy all the time. After a while I come to my senses and realize that removing all fear or sadness would dehumanize me. I'd become a kind of robot, incapable of living life to its fullest, even robbed of the ability to survive. I need to experience all human emotions, fear as well as joy, to successfully survive and thrive during unemployment. Instead of wishing my humanity away, I trust in God to strengthen me to meet whatever challenges await me.

God provides us with the emotional resources we need to survive unemployment and to find contentment and even joy in spite of our circumstances.

I will trust in God, my help, refuge, and strength.

Provision

Who provides for the raven its prey, when its young ones cry to God, and wander about for lack of food?
—Job 38:41

There is a Yiddish proverb that goes, "God will provide—if only God would provide until he provides." We all need a job and steady income again. We have no assurances of exactly when we will find work, but we are sure that God will love and care for us during unemployment. God will give us just what we need to live for the moment.

Each day is filled with small victories that promote our survival. Those victories are the signs of the provision of God. I regularly look for those signs during unemployment: God gives me this day my daily bread, the roof over my head, my health, energy to keep looking for a job, friends and family who love me, as well as a little money from unemployment insurance. Sure I want more. I want to find a job and to stop worrying about money. But that will happen eventually, not now. For now, God has given me what I need to live today.

Today is important because today is all we really have. We will work again, but in the meantime the same God who provides food for the birds will provide for us. We hope in God who "provides until he provides."

God is the source of all I need for today. Evidence of God's care and love is all around me right now.

Everything for Our Enjoyment

As for those who in the present age are rich, command them
not to be haughty, or to set their hopes on the uncertainty
of riches, but rather on God who richly provides
us with everything for our enjoyment.
—1 Timothy 6:17

God not only provides what is necessary to survive but also gives
to us "everything for our enjoyment." If we are unemployed now or
find our present jobs unsatisfying, we are still able to identify those
"little extras" that let us know God is good.

So many anxieties cloud our vision regarding work or lack of
work that it becomes difficult to discern what gifts from God bring
us enjoyment. But those little extras are there if we take the time each
day to see them and touch them. Being unemployed or hating our
jobs makes it easy to believe that there is not enough in our lives to
live on, but God has provided us with more than enough to appreciate life right now. We can still enjoy the smile on a child's face, the
companionship of a pet, the kiss of a spouse, or a hug from a friend.
We can still enjoy the beauty of a sunset, the music of a choir, or the
joy of participating in worship.

Today meditate for fifteen minutes or more in a house of worship. Look around and associate things you see in God's house with
blessings in your life—blessings that bring you joy daily. Say a prayer
of thanks to God, who gives you true riches no matter how poor you
seem to be.

God has given me everything for my enjoyment today.

Our Hearts' Desires

**Take delight in the Lord, and he will give you
the desires of your heart.**
—Psalm 37:4

Sometimes it's hard to know the desires of our own hearts. One of the keys to discovering our hearts' desires is a willingness to ask ourselves, "What am I learning during unemployment? What do I know about myself now that I didn't know when I was working?" I learned to delight in what God gives me today. I discovered that when I delight in what God gives me, like a roof over my head, food on the table, and loved ones. I am more in touch with what I want out of life—peace and contentment. And I trust that God will supply me employment that in some way will add to the peace and contentment I desire.

Another way to learn our hearts' desires is to find a way to let those hidden desires surface into our conscious minds. I have a friend who recently started to meditate for a brief time each day. When he first began the practice, all that he wanted from God was a new job. But as he continued to meditate week after week, he found that getting a new job was not his highest priority after all. Instead what he wanted most out of life was to spend more time with his family. He realized he delighted most in God when he was at home. Now he is looking for a job that offers either part-time or flex-time hours. Realizing this shift in life priorities was a tremendous relief for my friend, and he brings to his job search renewed passion and energy for a different kind of job than the one he thought he wanted.

We can use a variety of means to take delight in the Lord and search the desires hidden in our hearts. Each desire we discover will help us focus on finding a job that allows us to express that desire.

*Today I will seek the desires of my heart and
delight in the Lord my God.*